I0427292

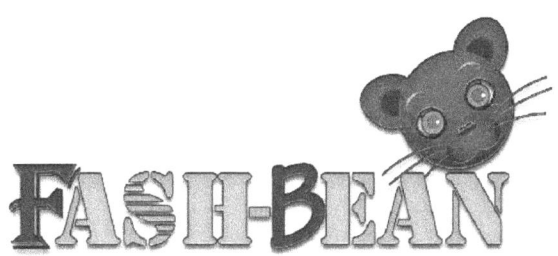

Author name: nk velu
About an author:
The author is a fashion designer, a graphic designer,
a content writer.
He has more than 20 years of experience in the field
of a fashion and apparel manufacturing. At present,
he is setting up his startup business in India and
the US. In the meantime, he wrote fiction and
non-fiction books for every one that interested him
and his readers, gave them stress relief, and
developed their mindset.

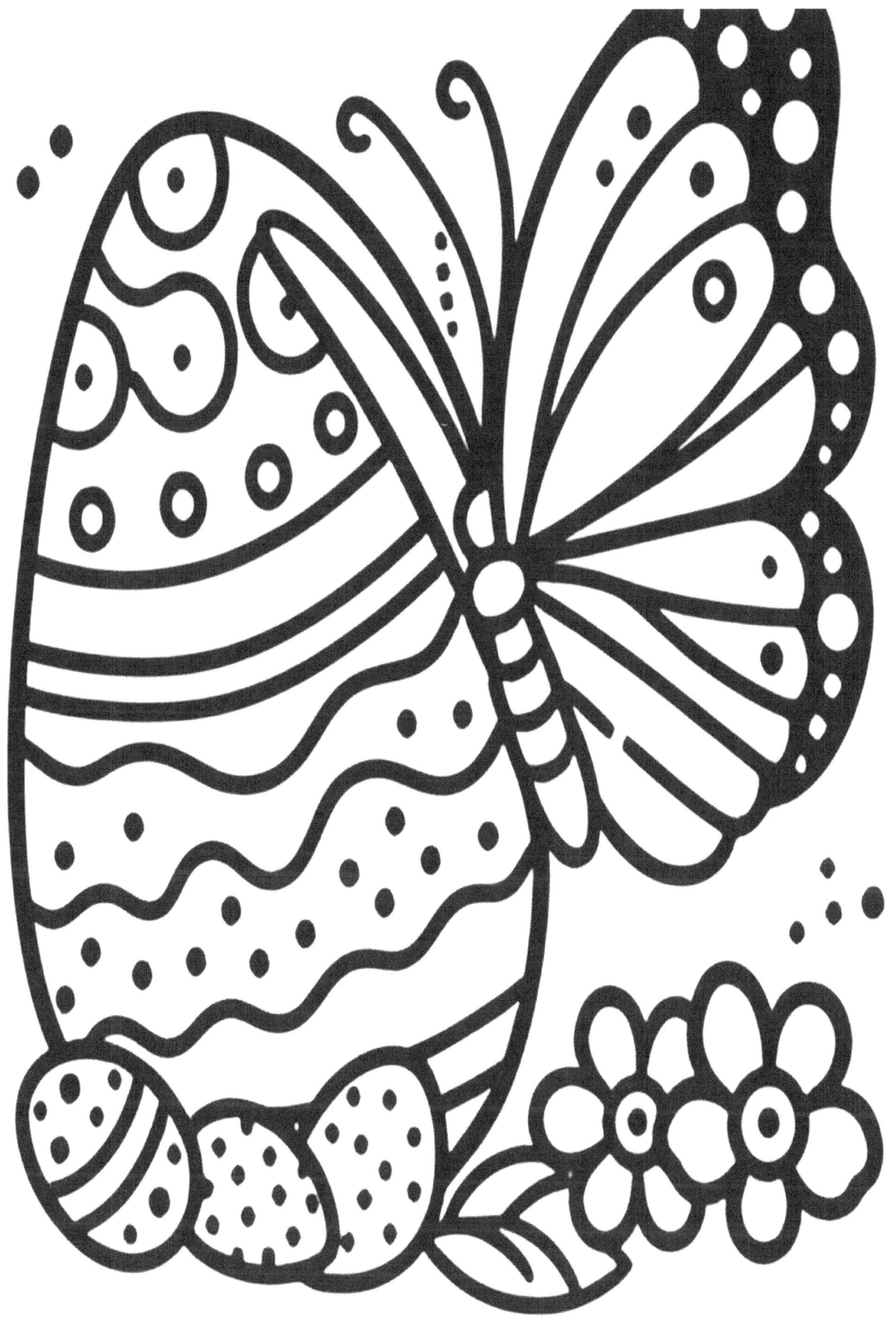

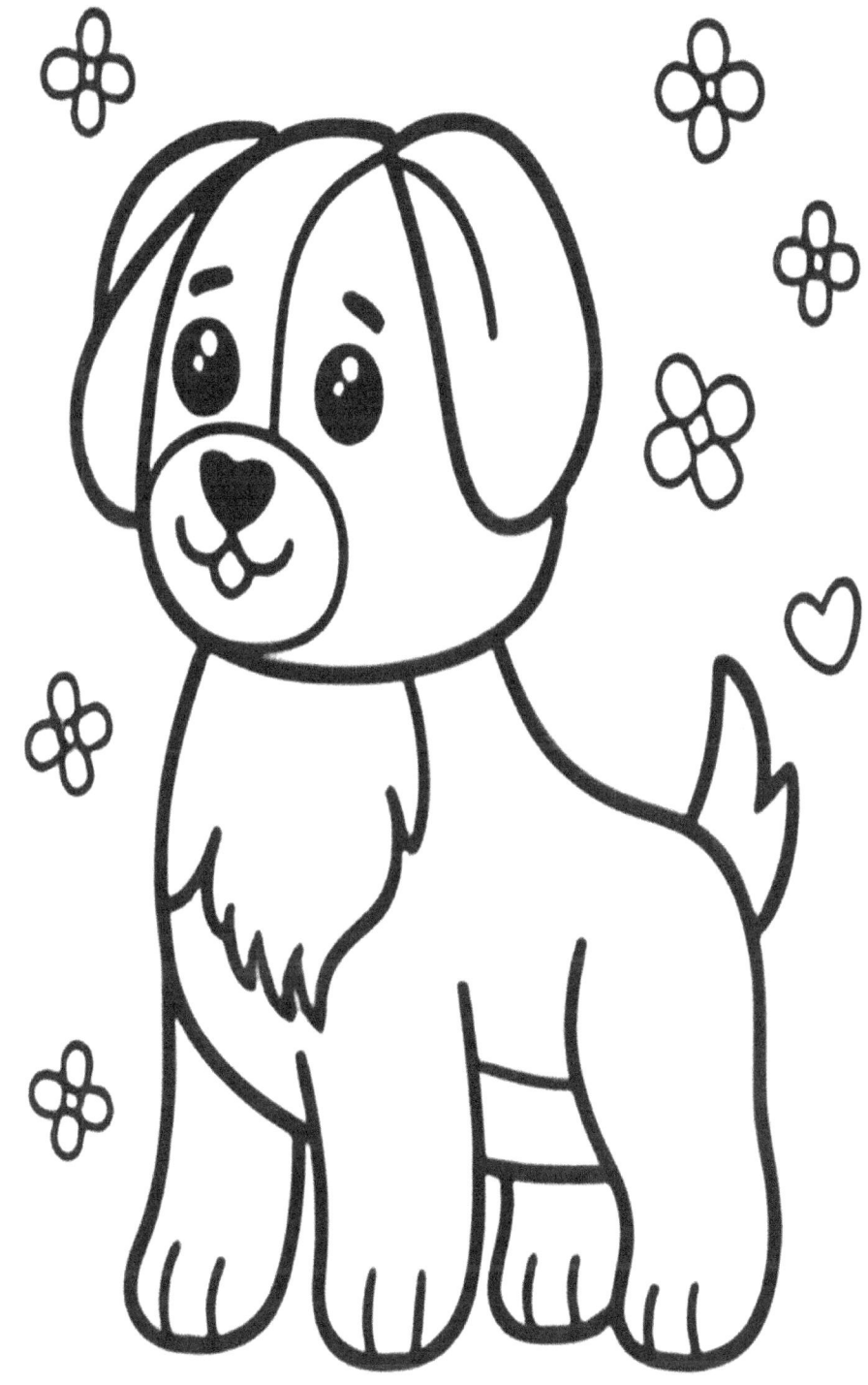

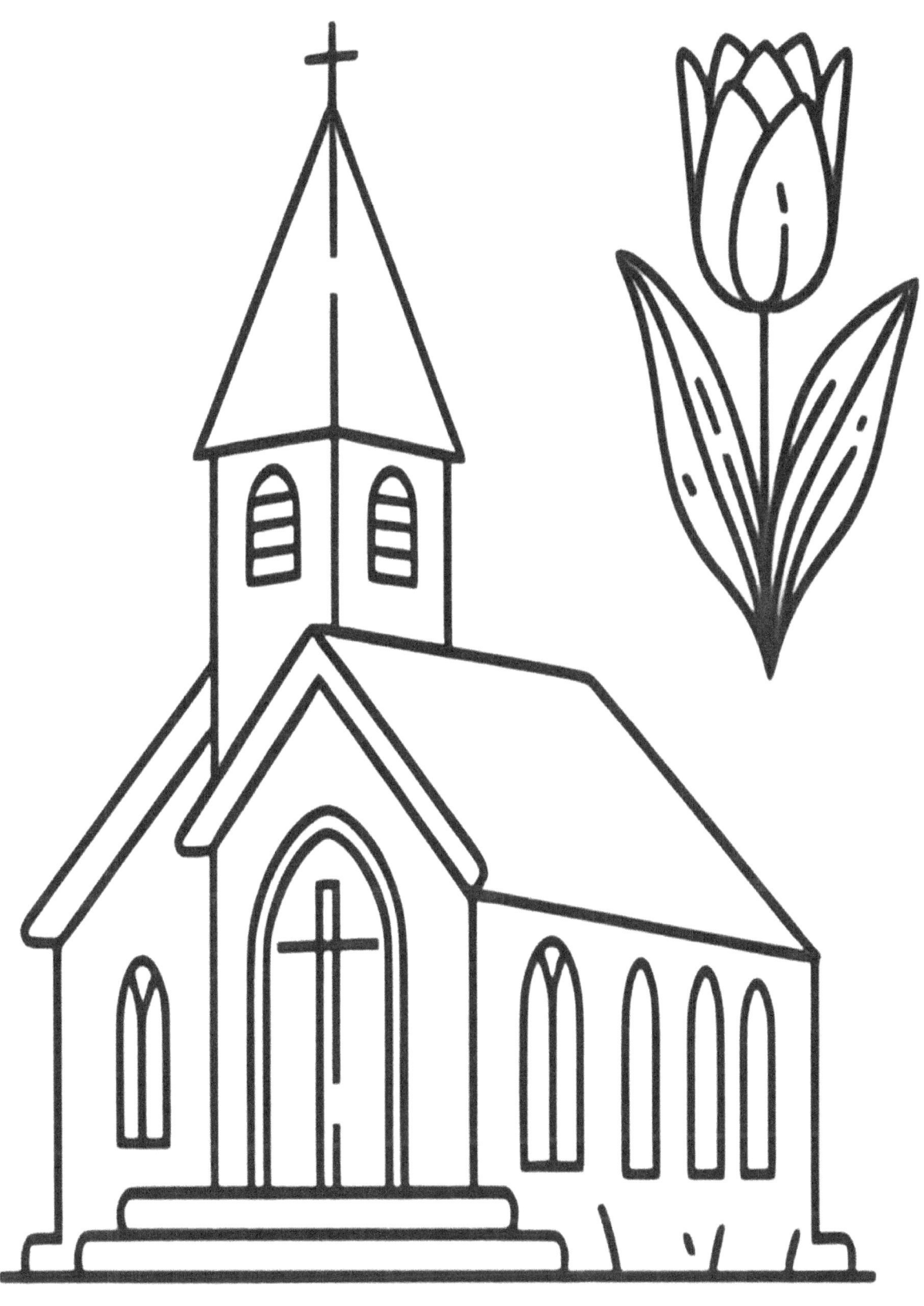

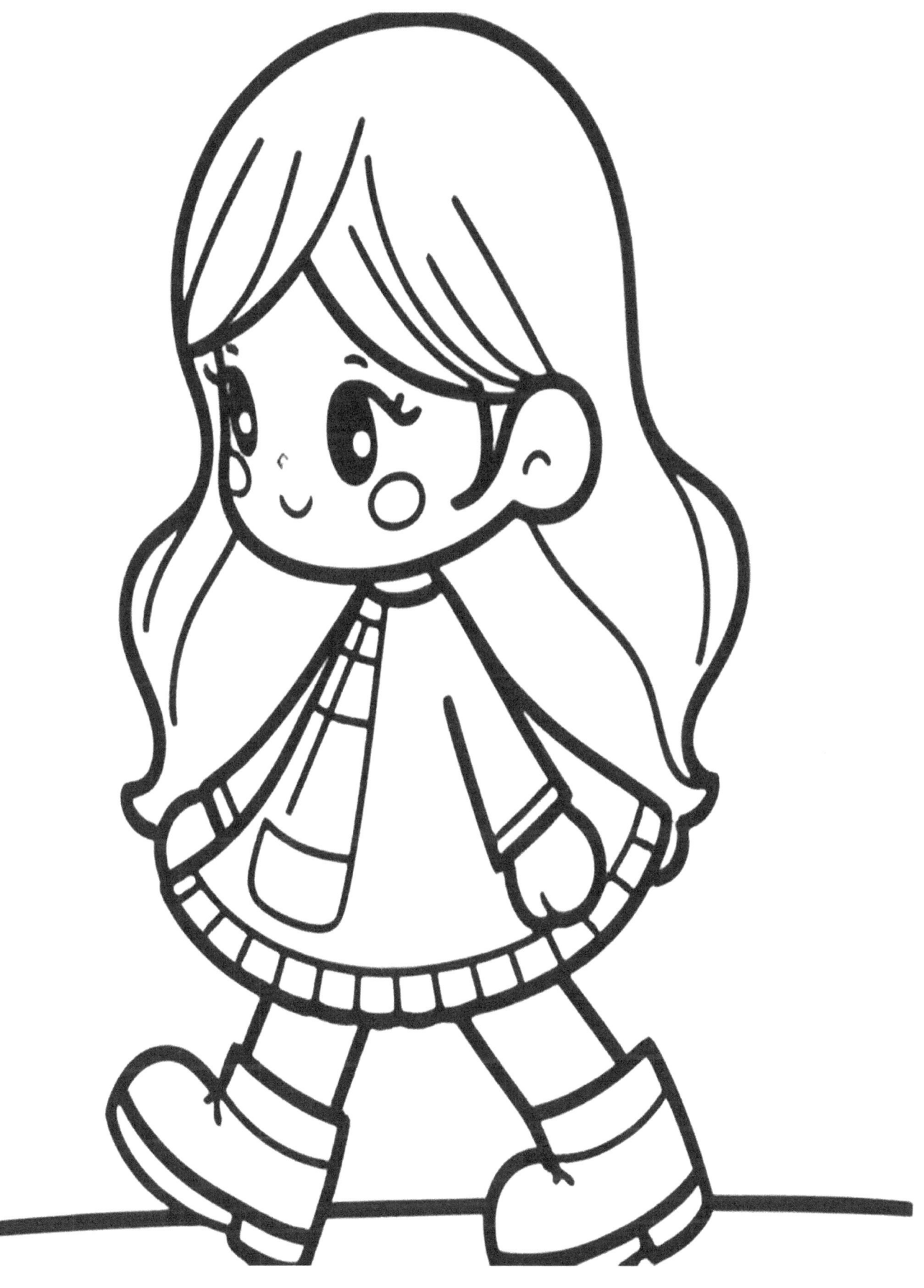

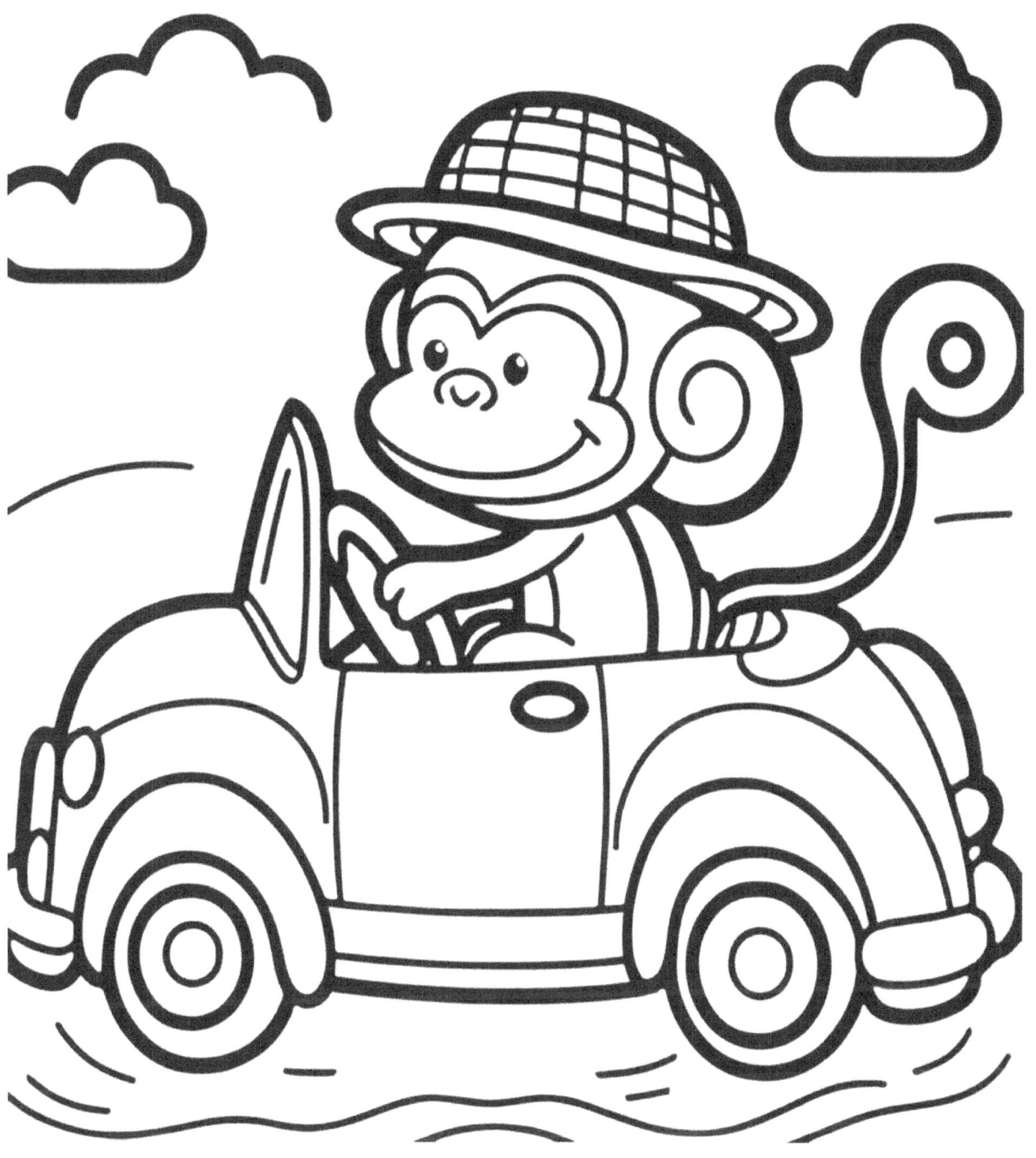

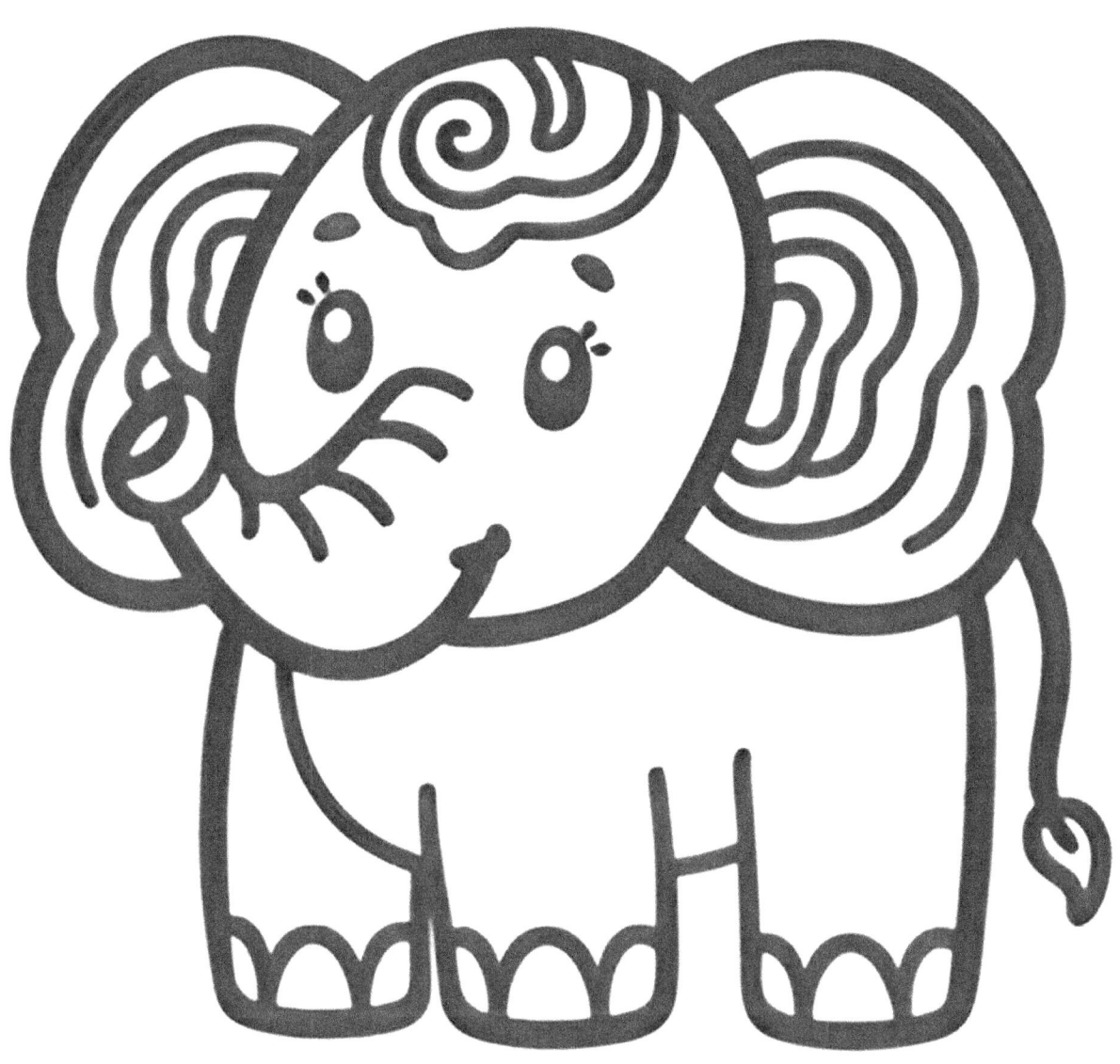

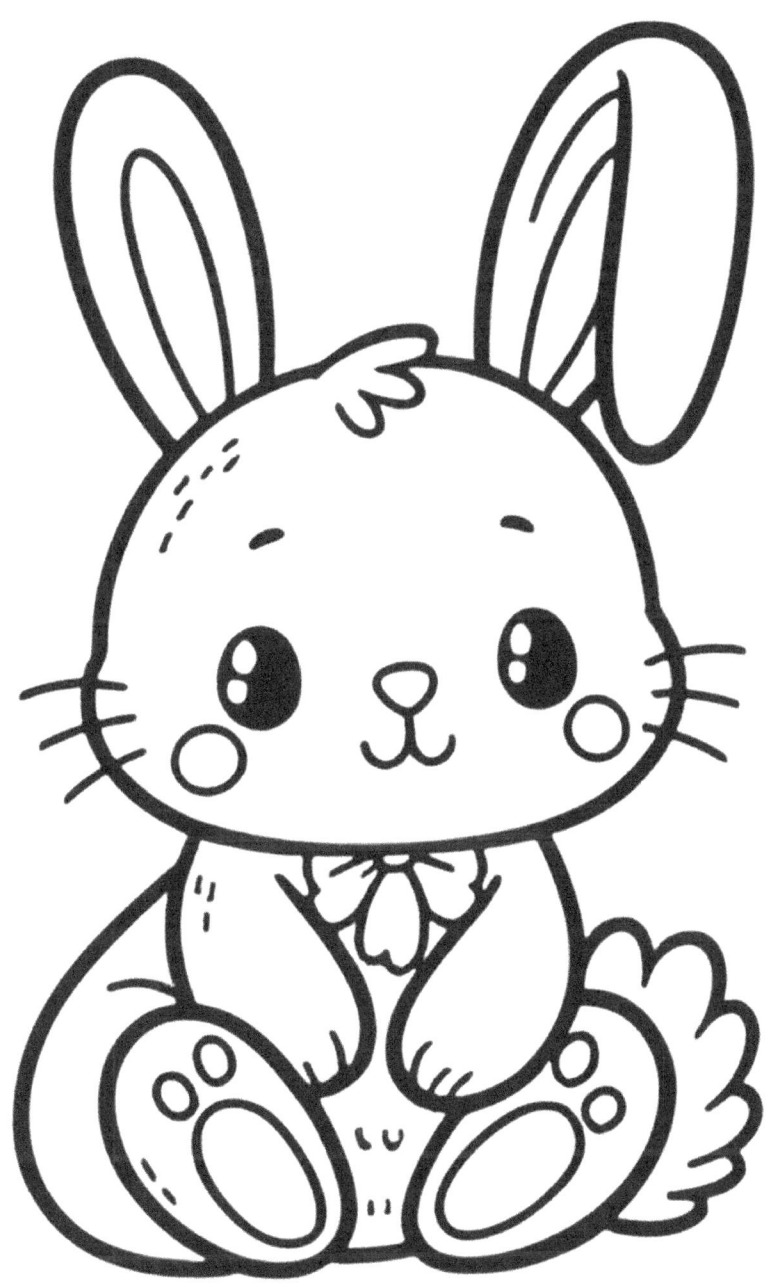

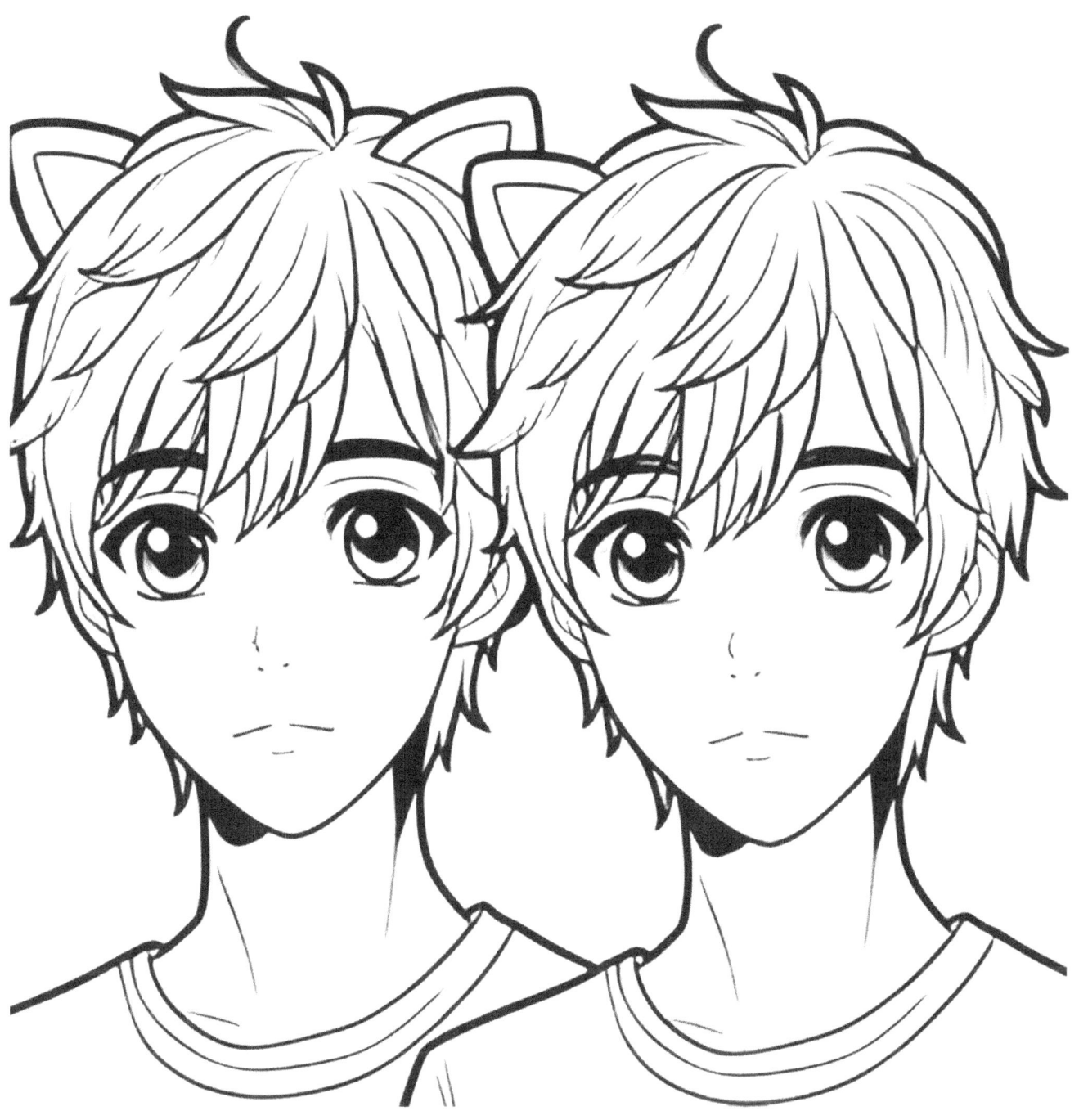

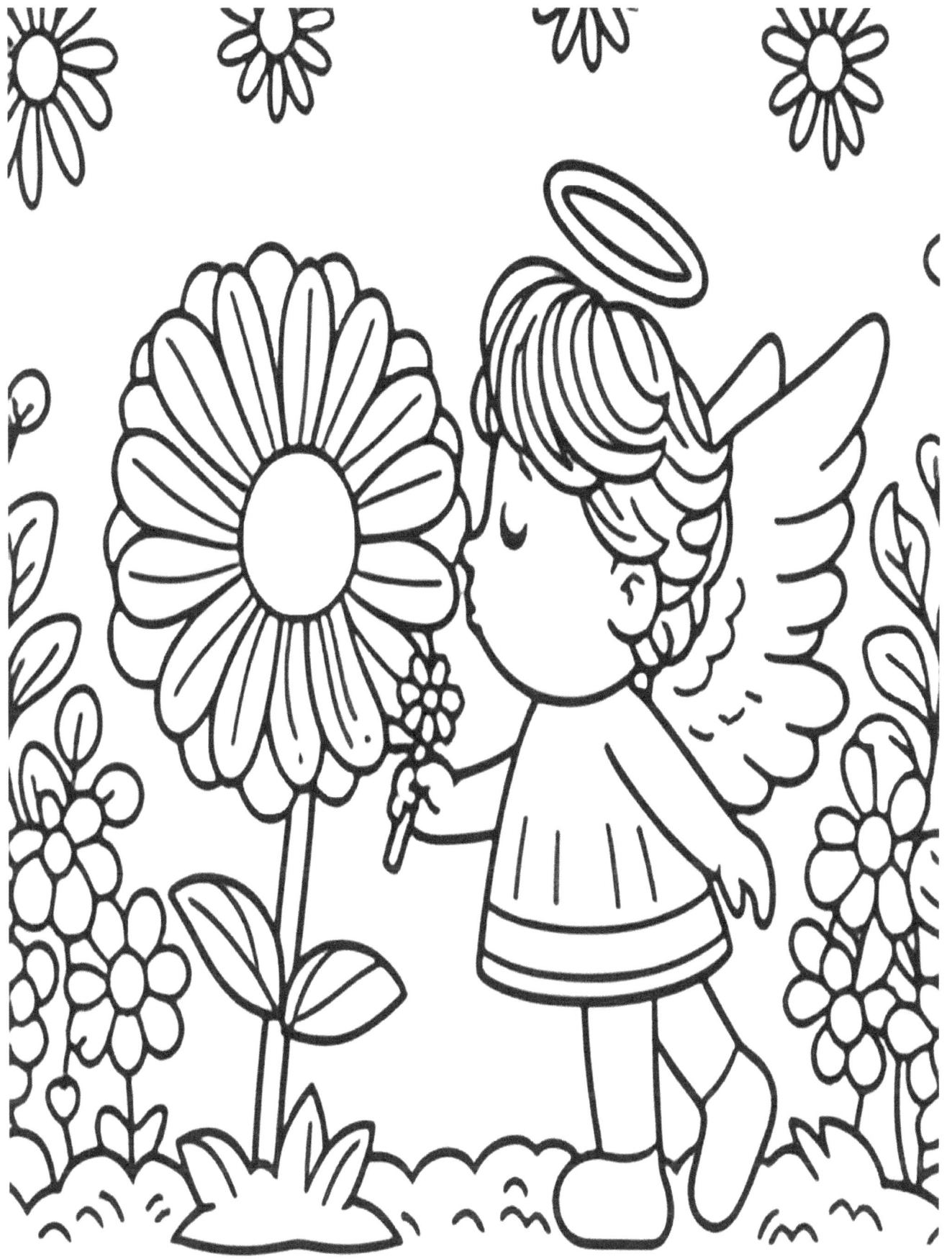

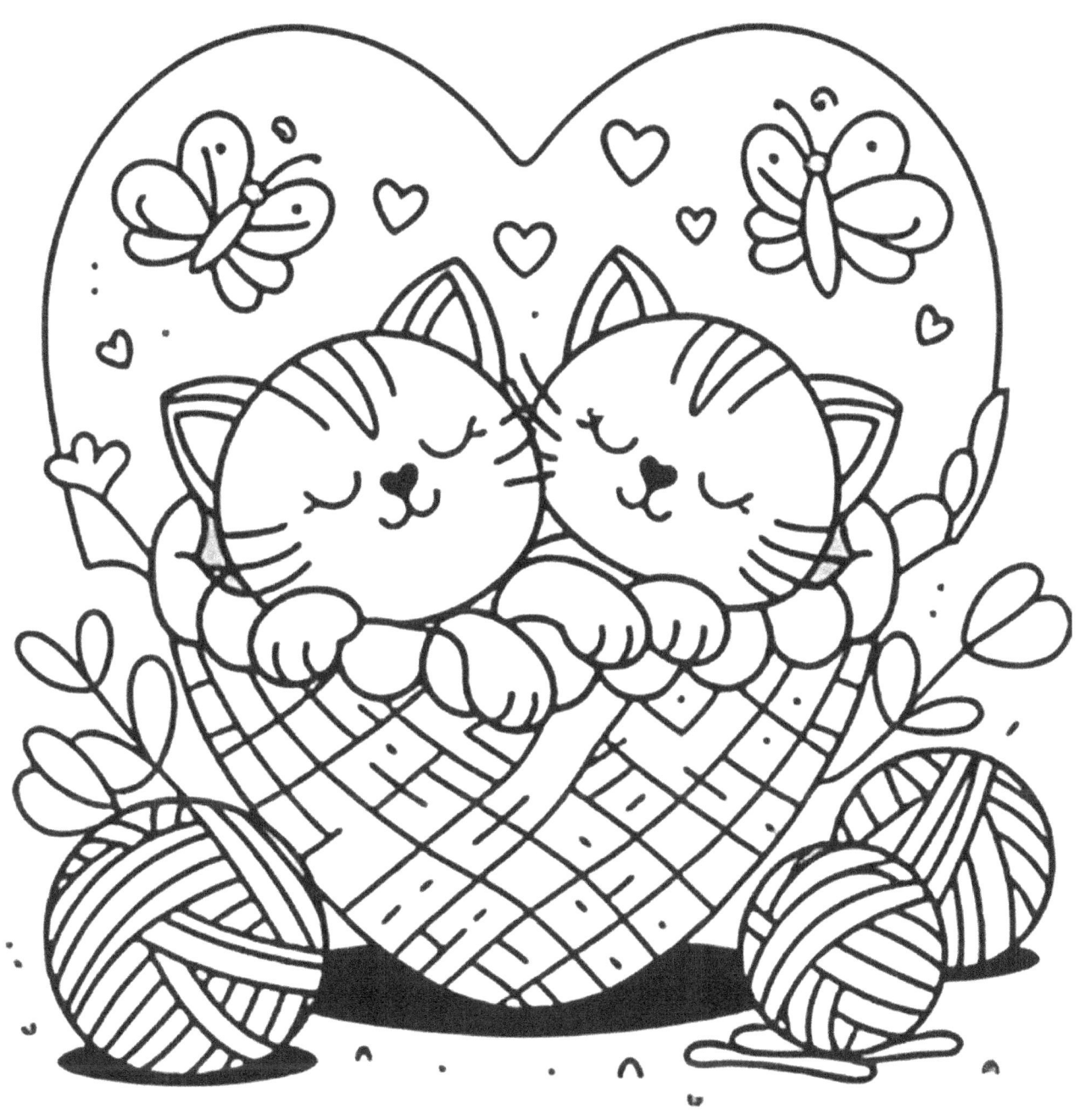

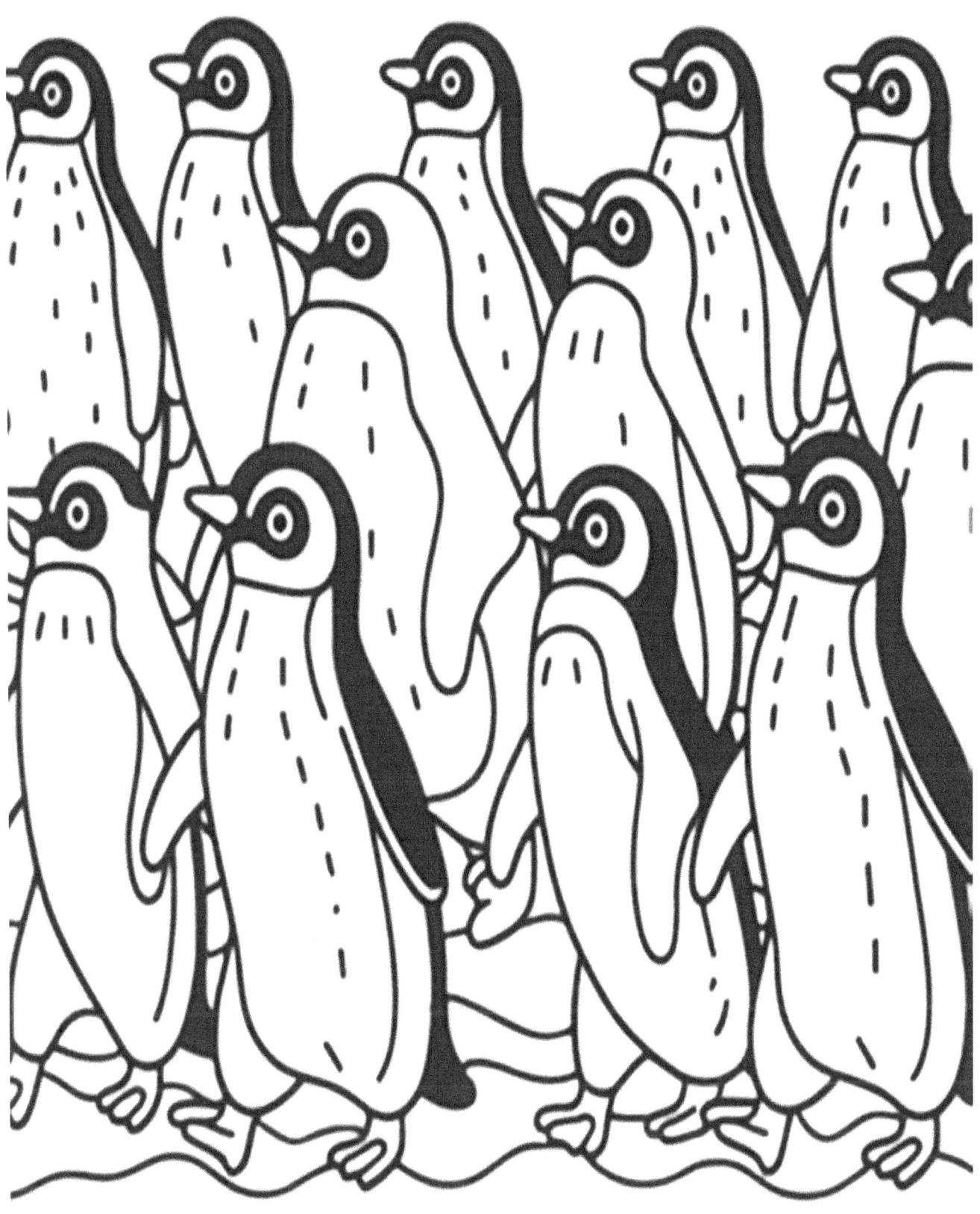

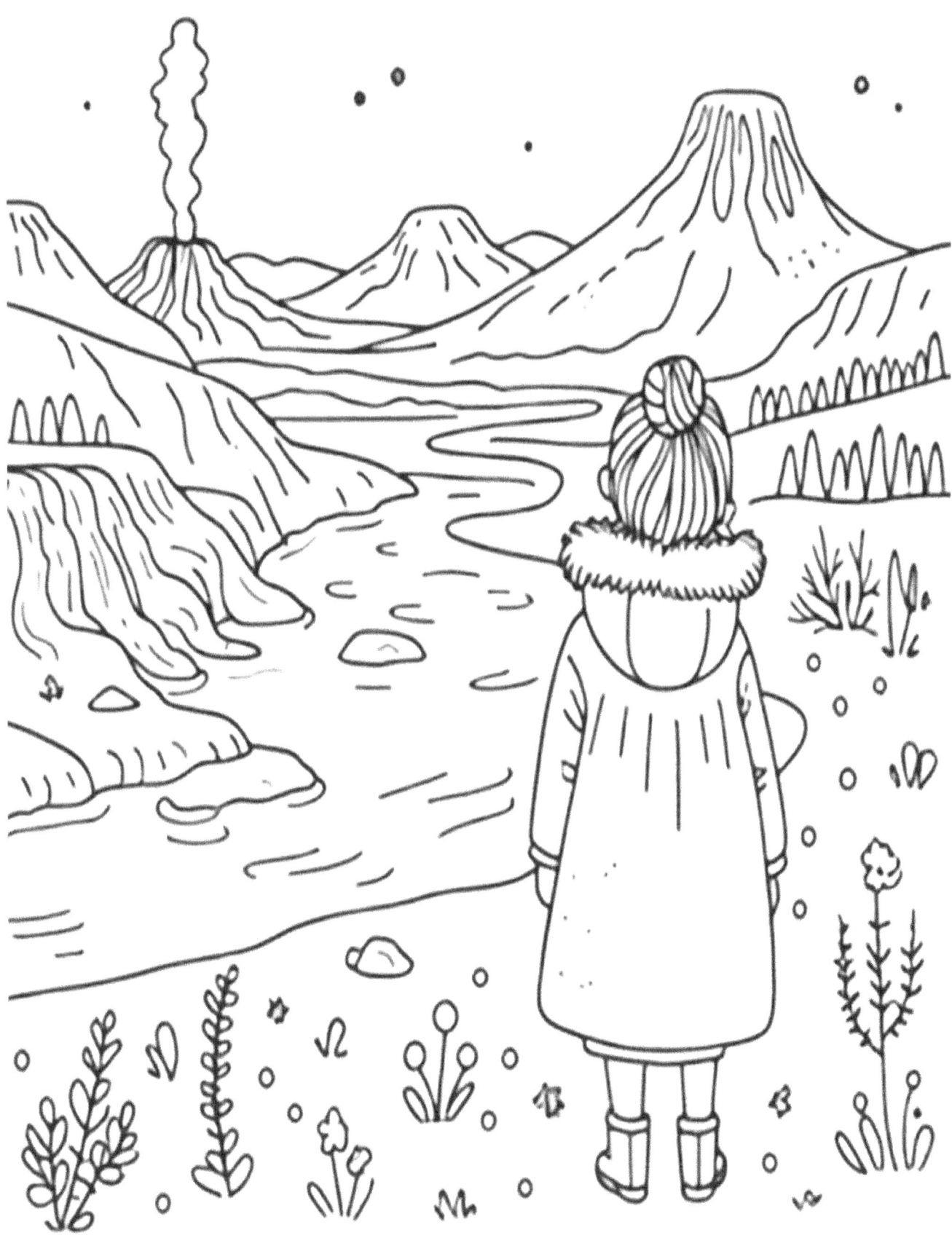

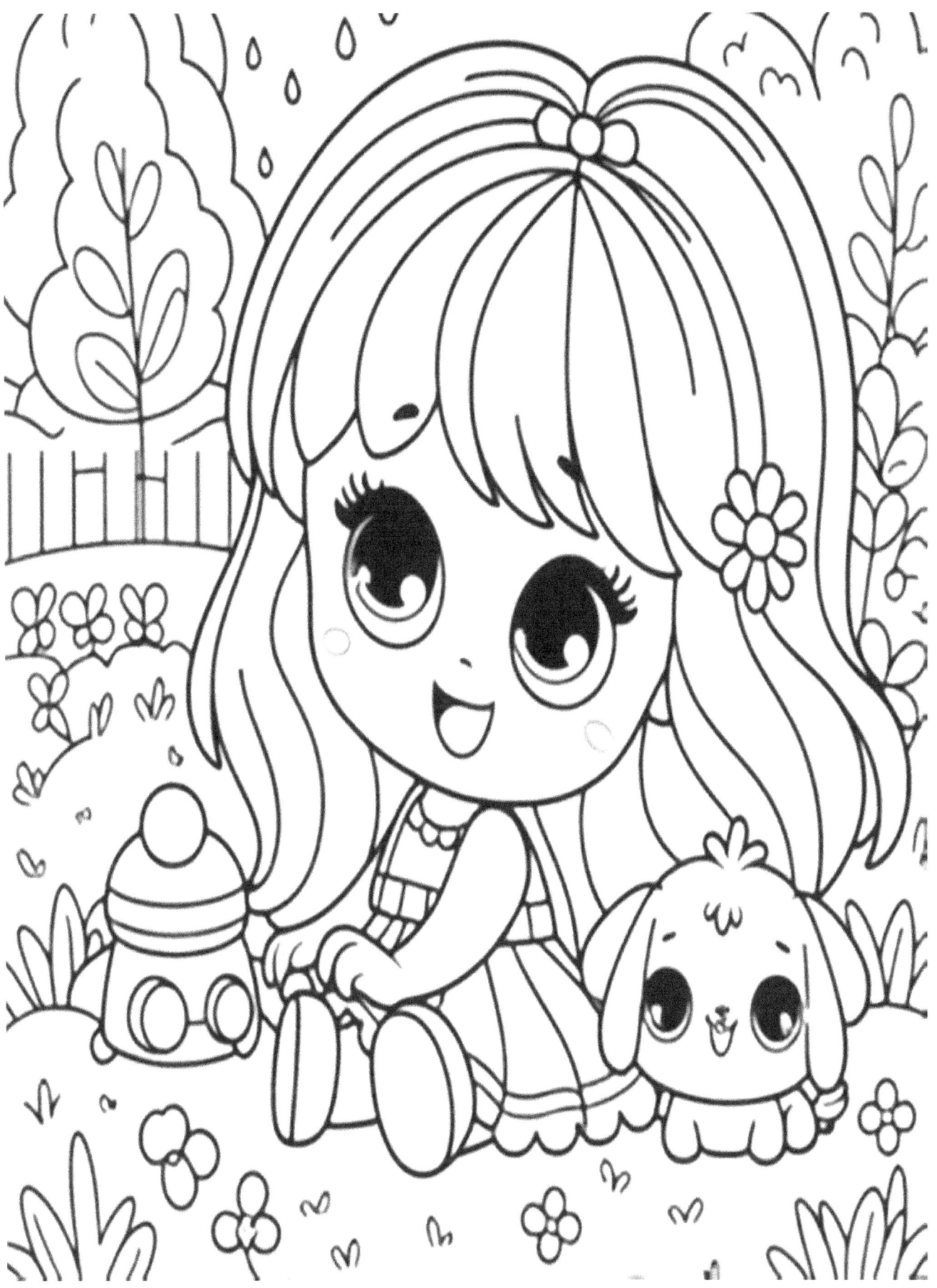

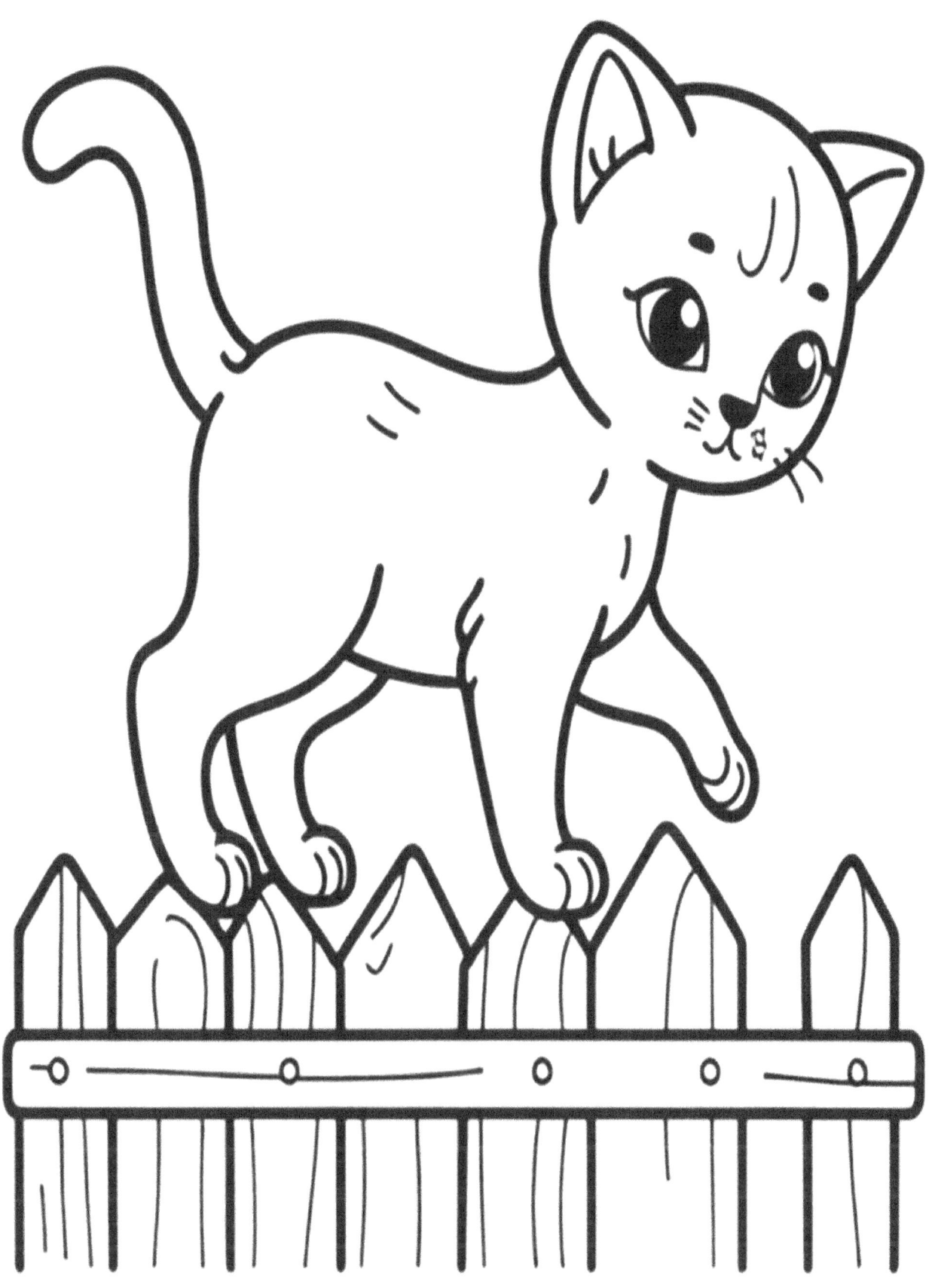

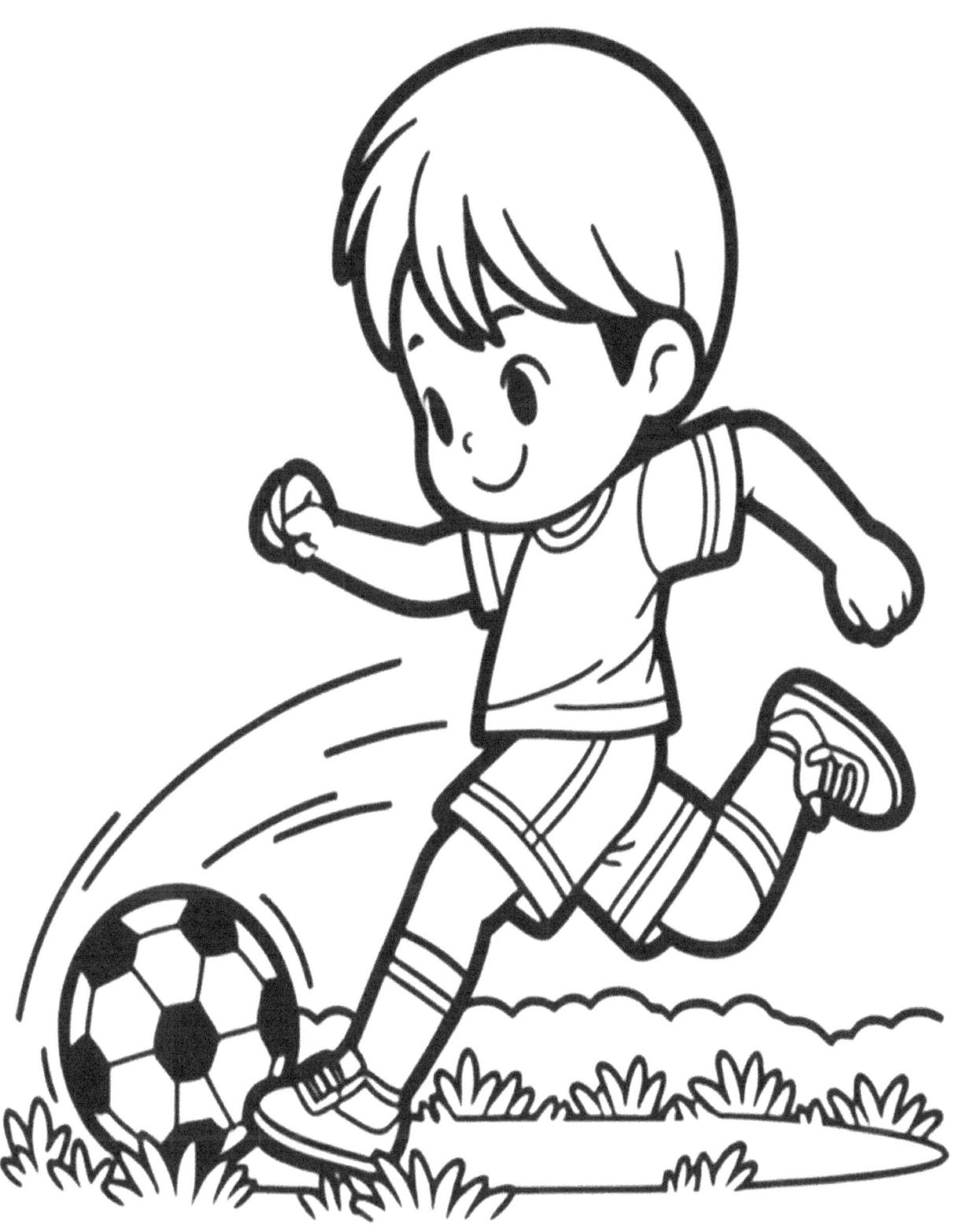

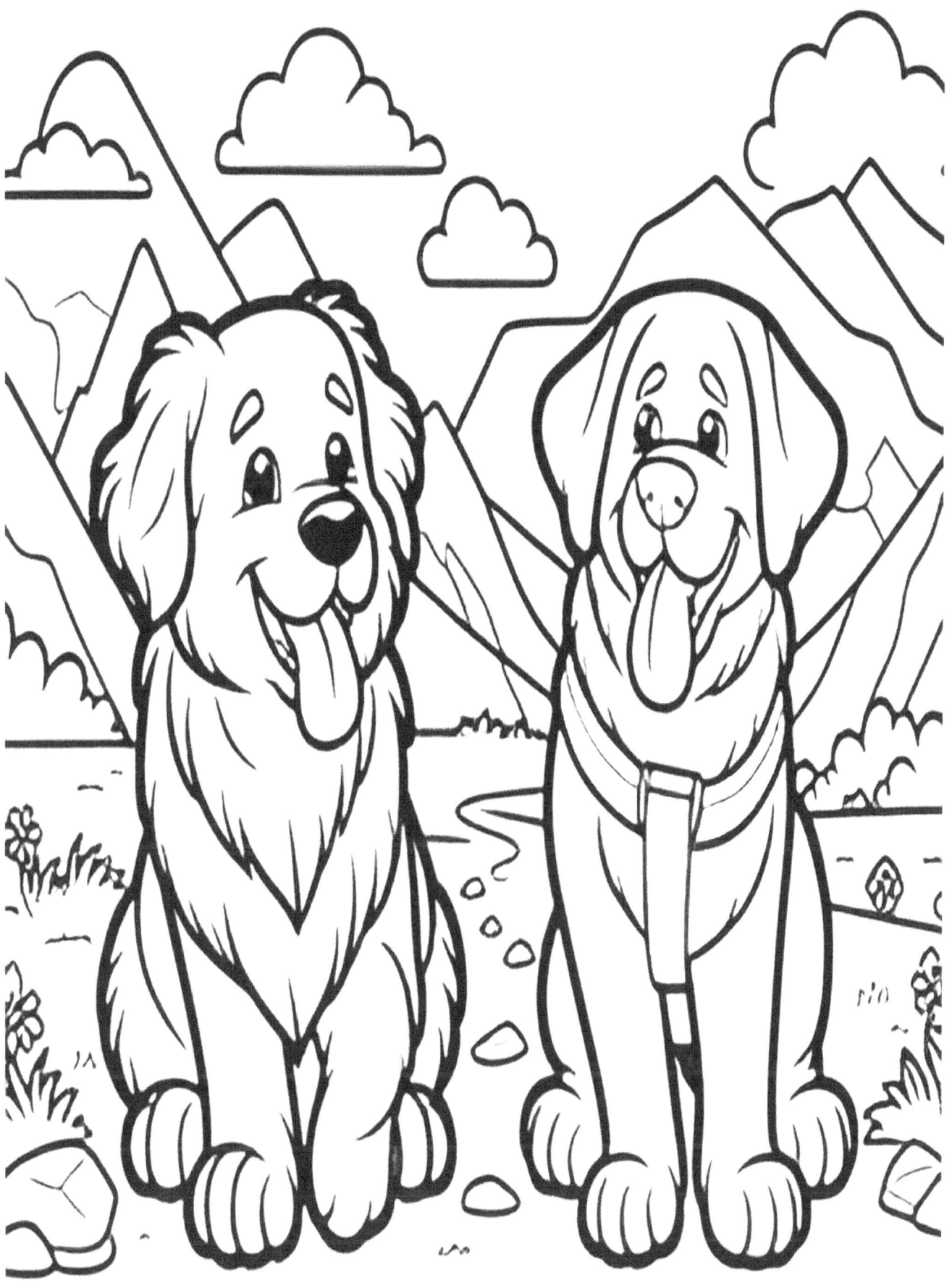

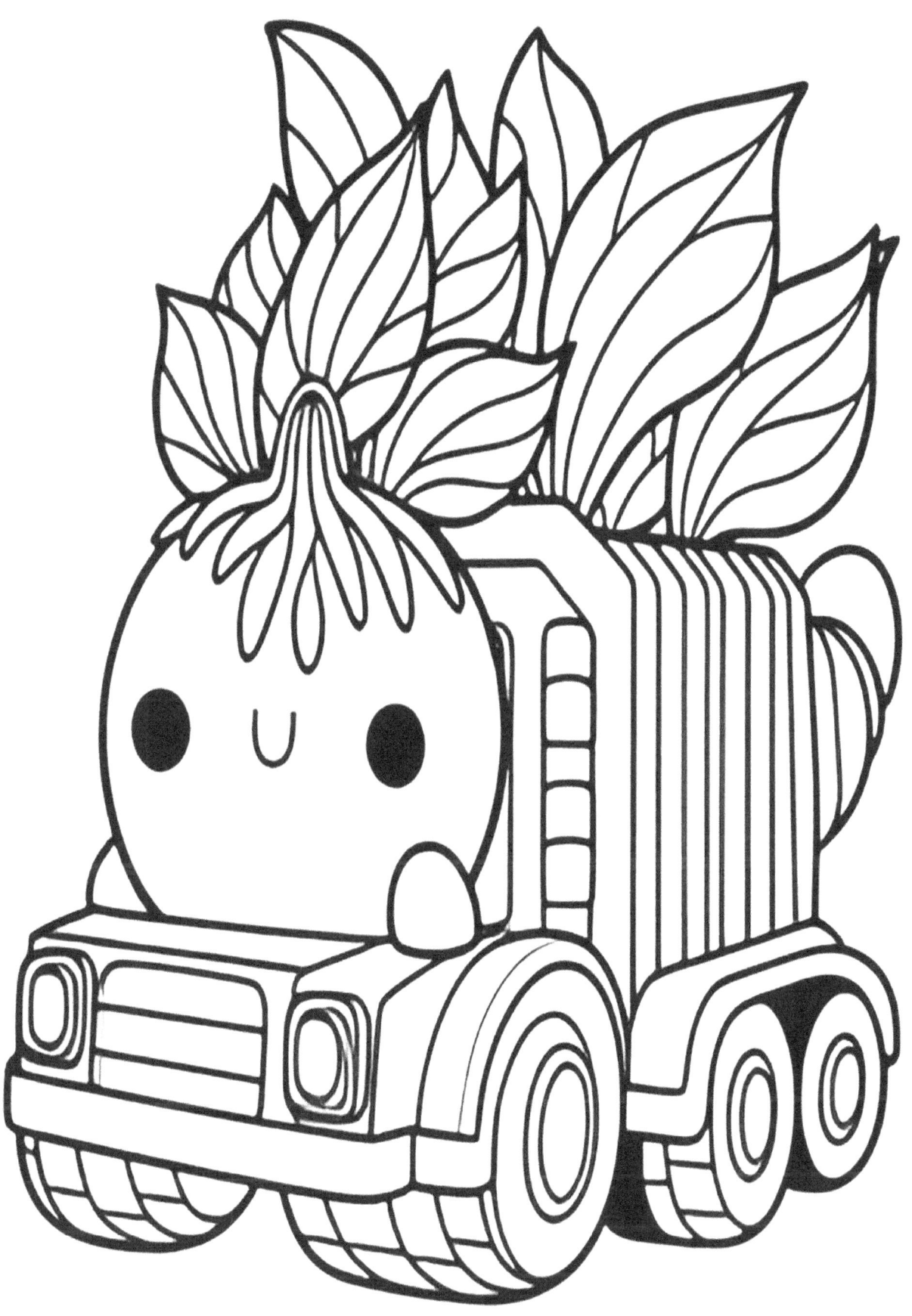

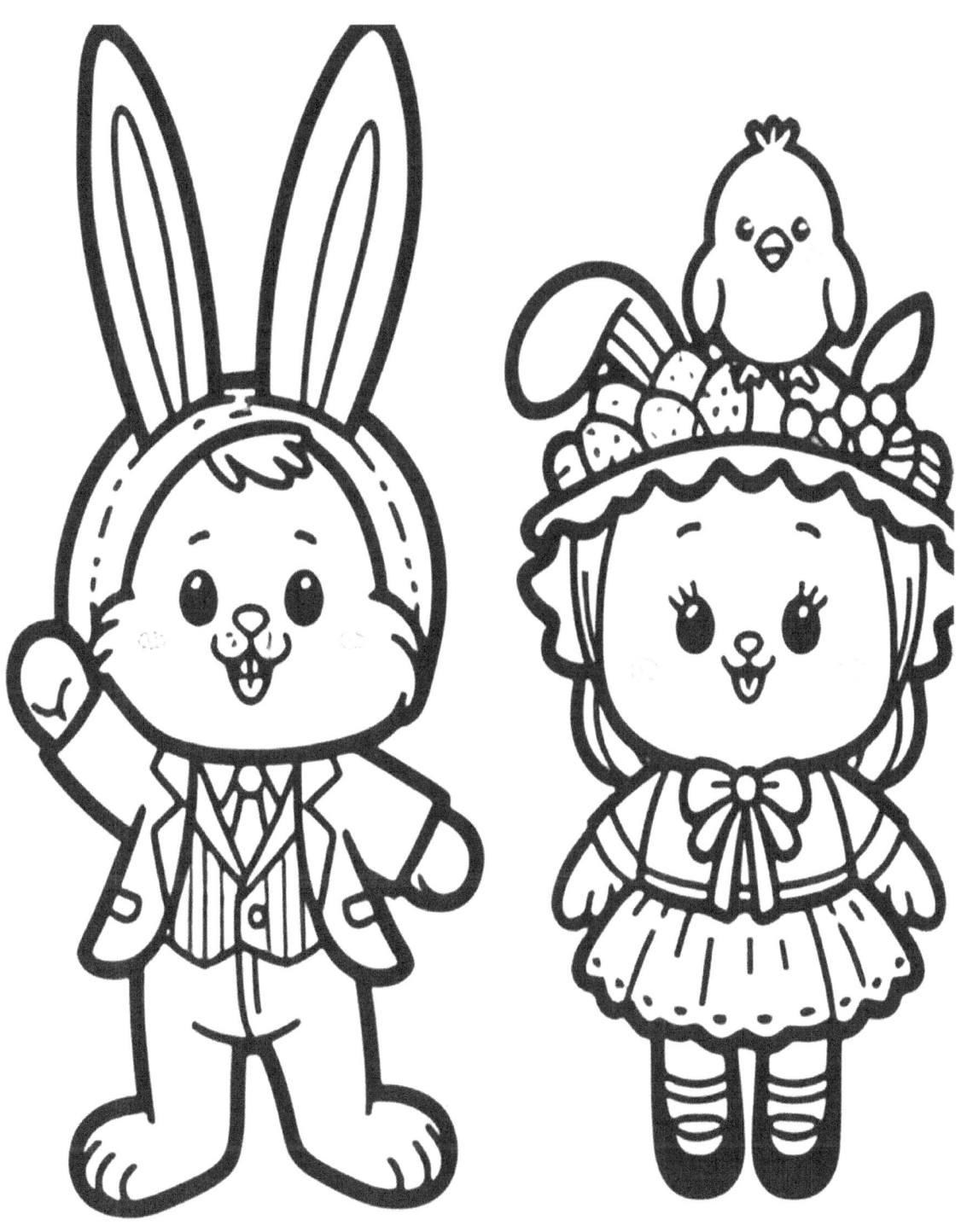

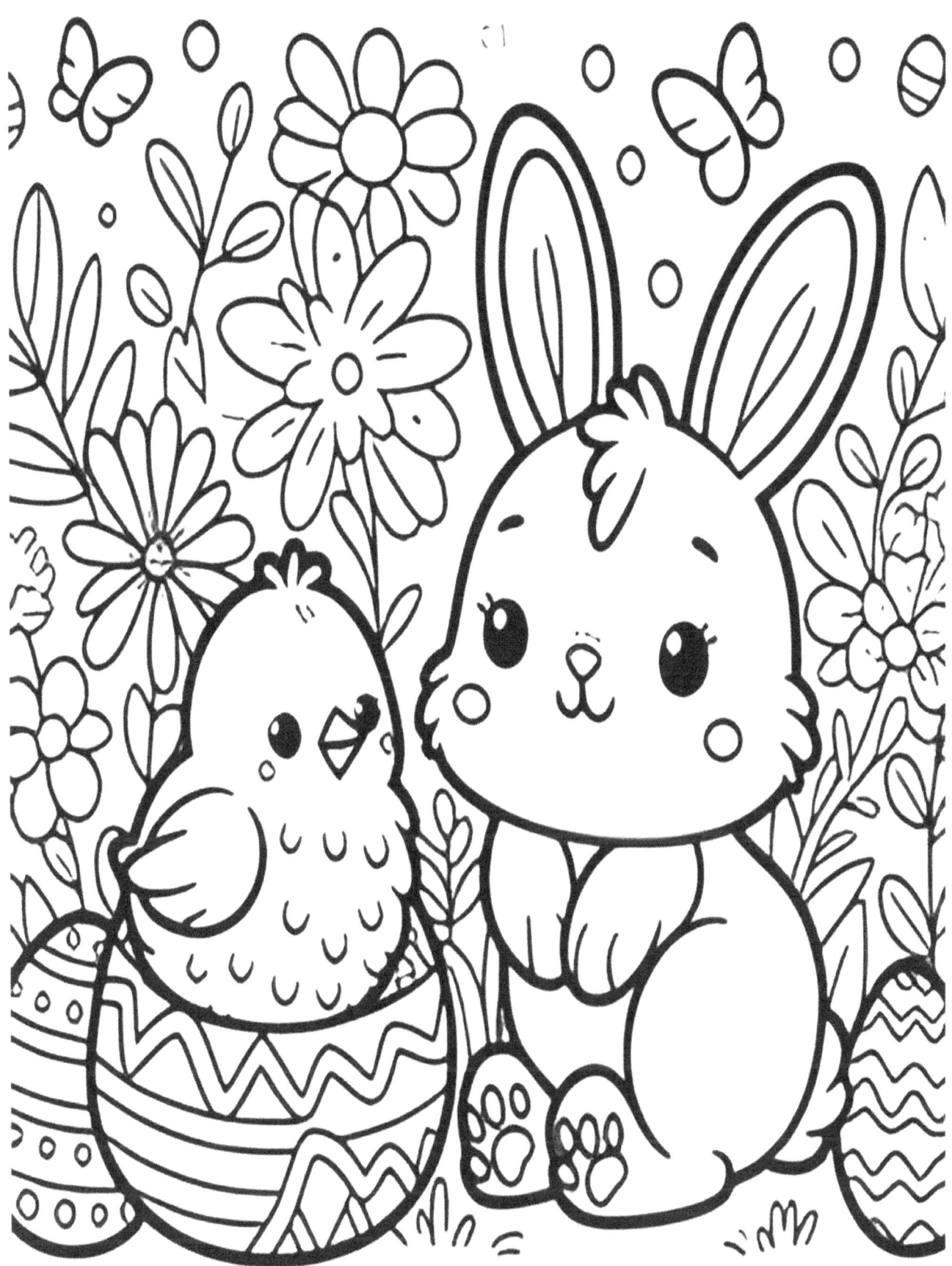

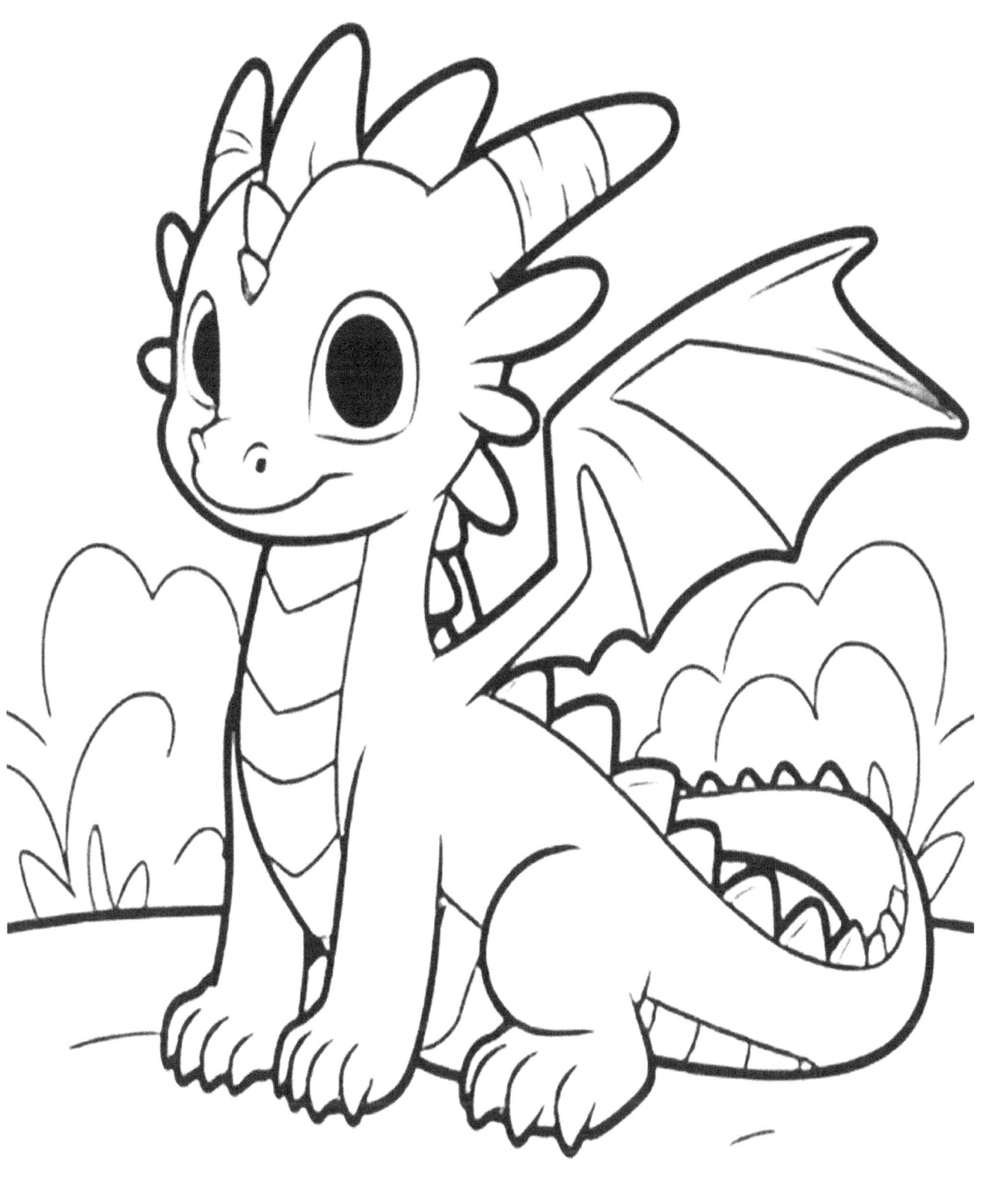

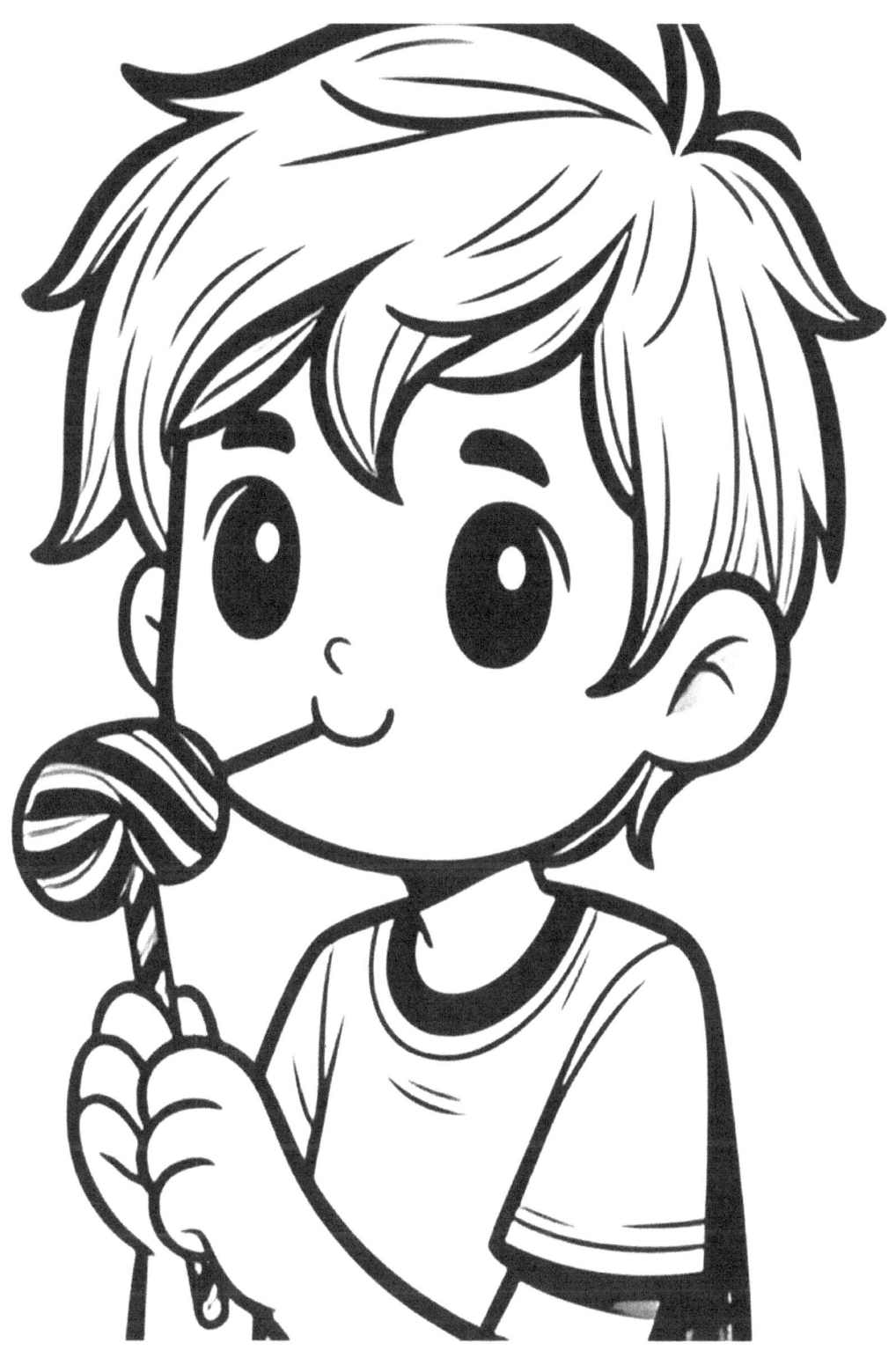

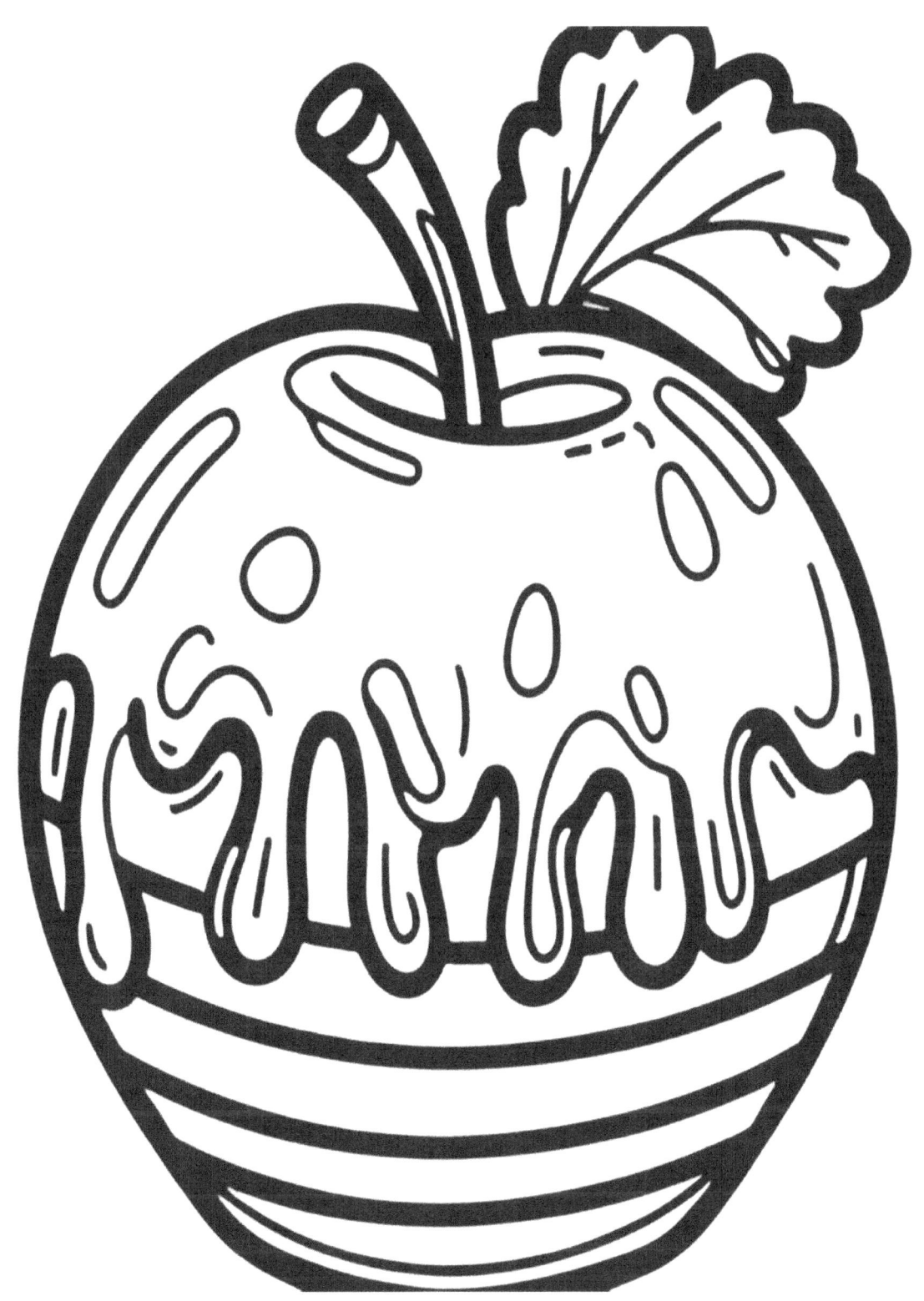

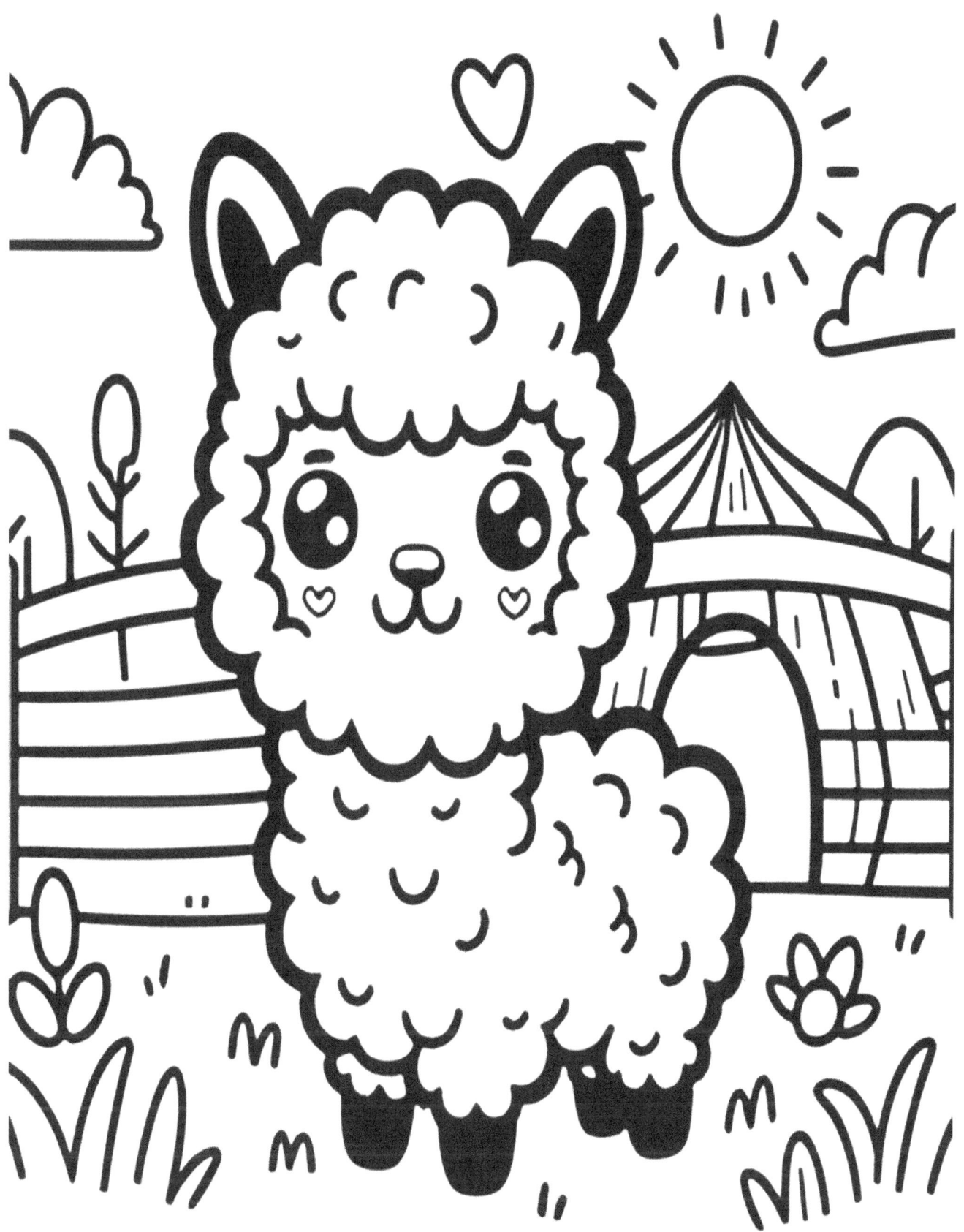

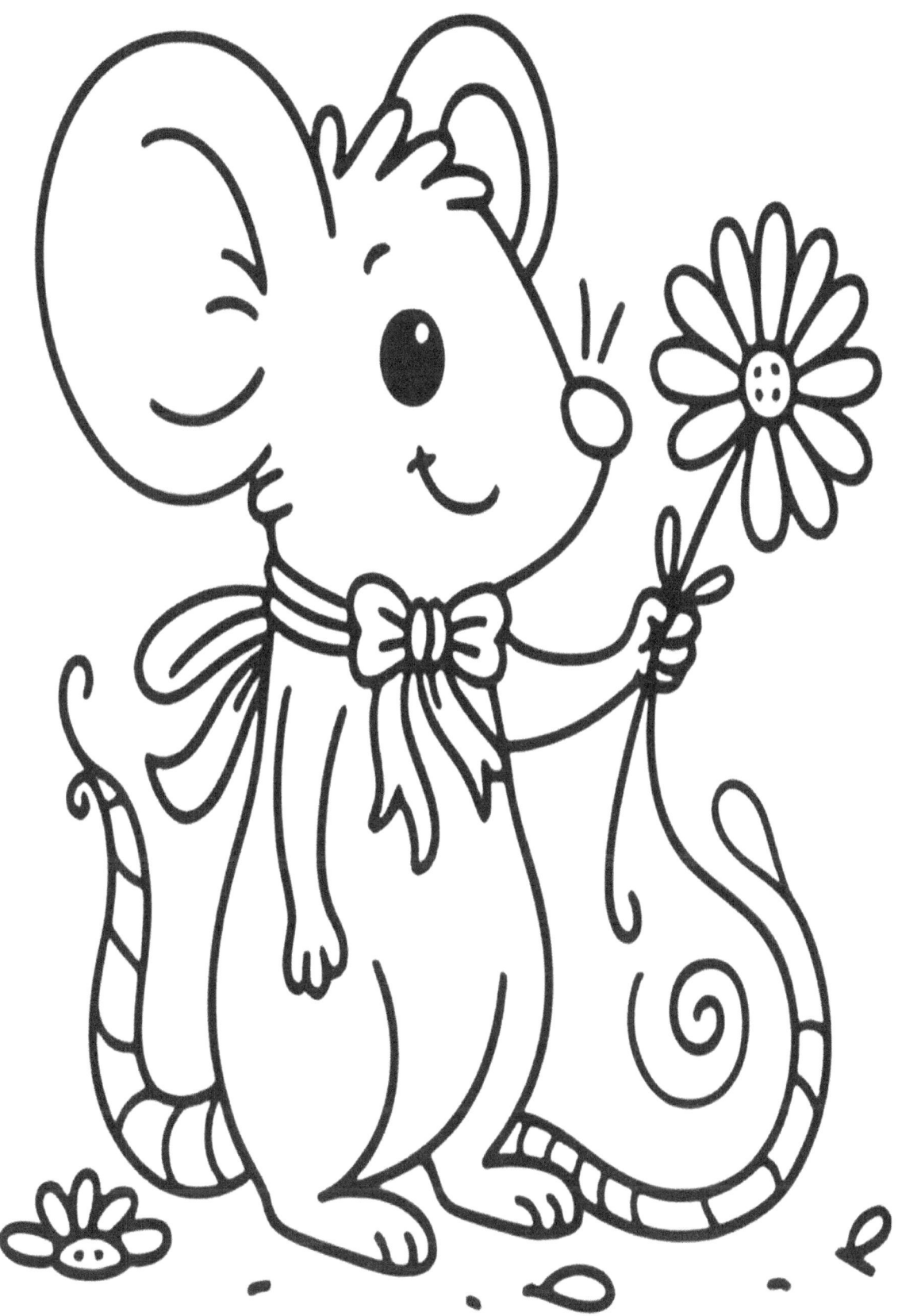

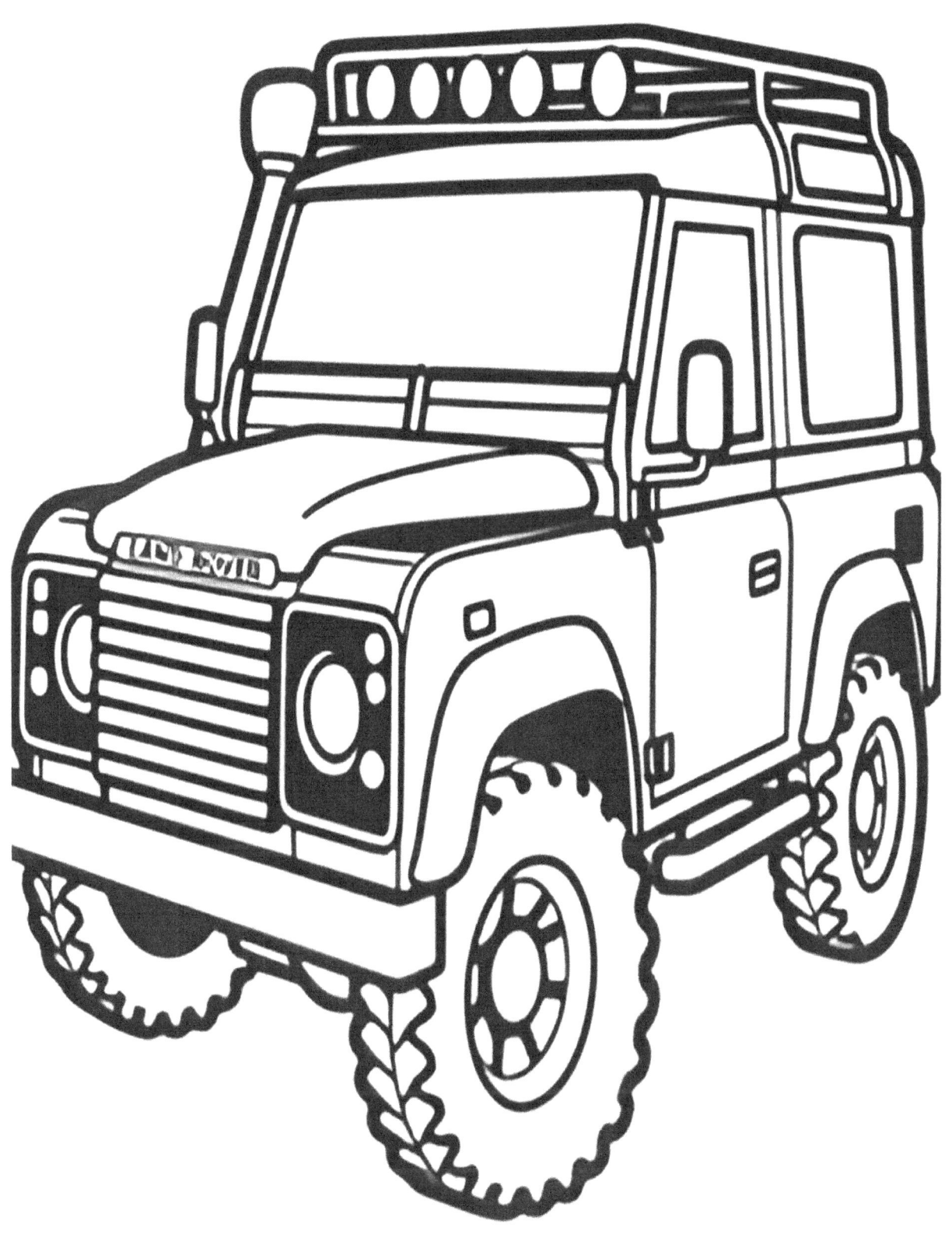

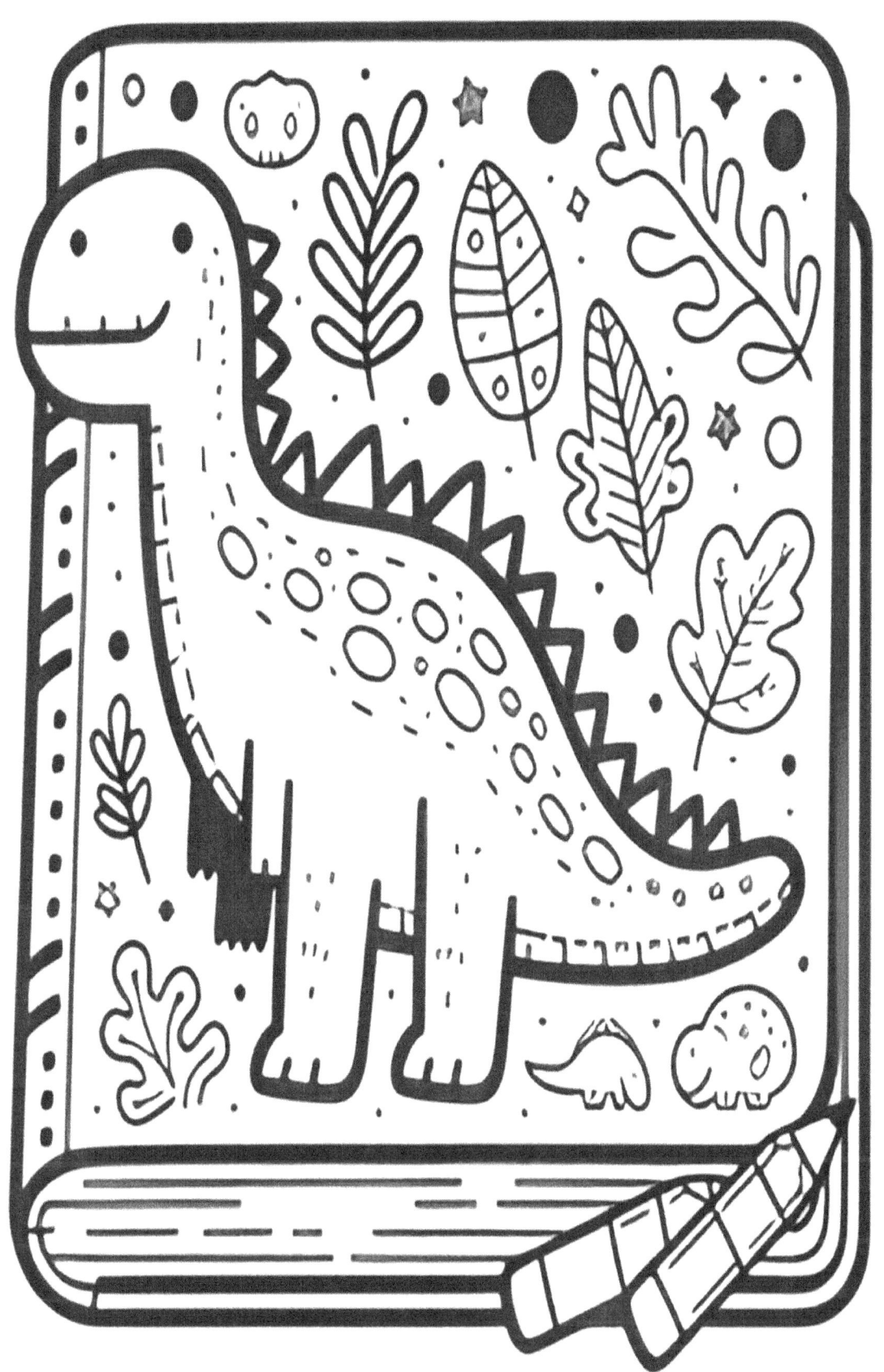

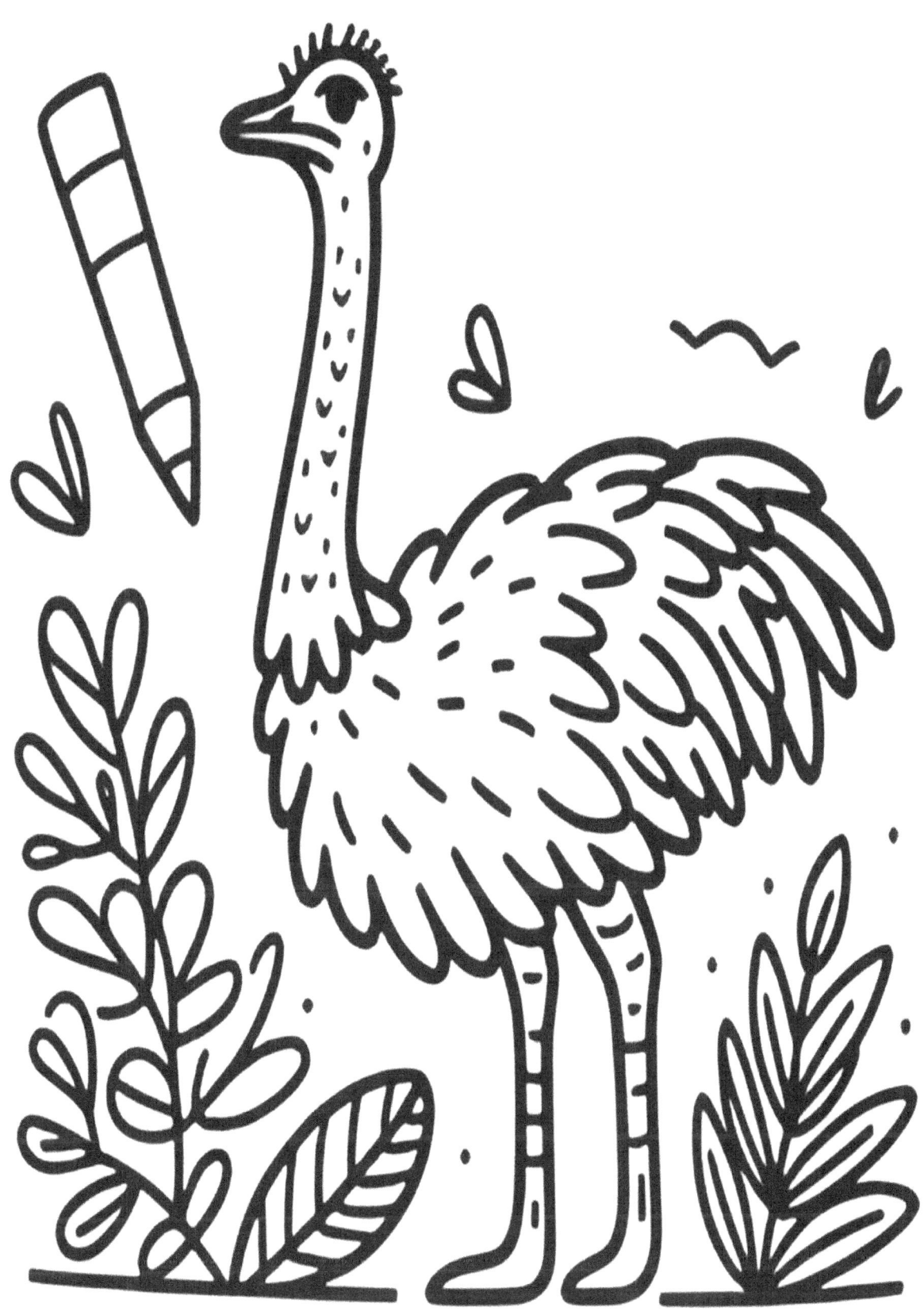

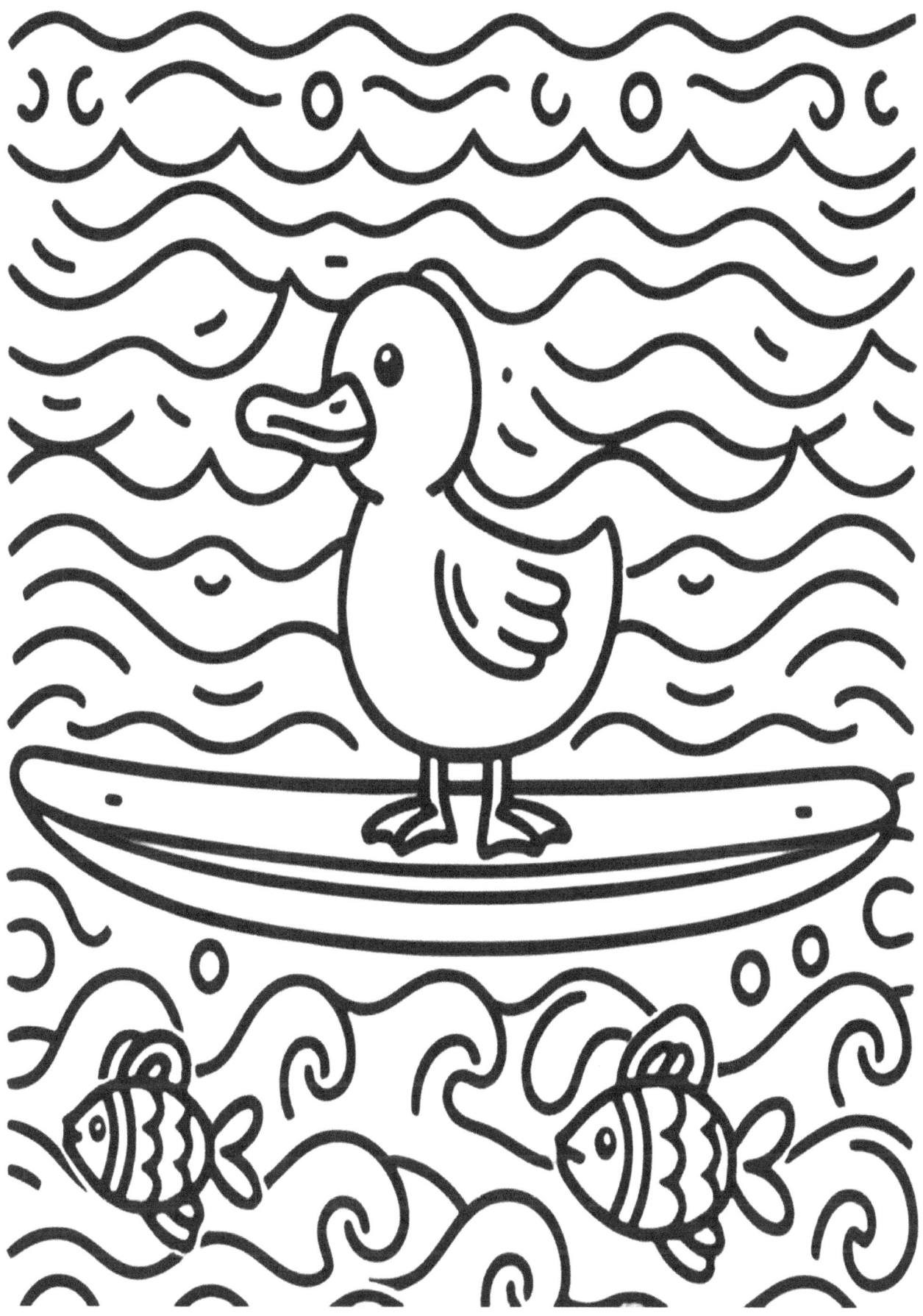

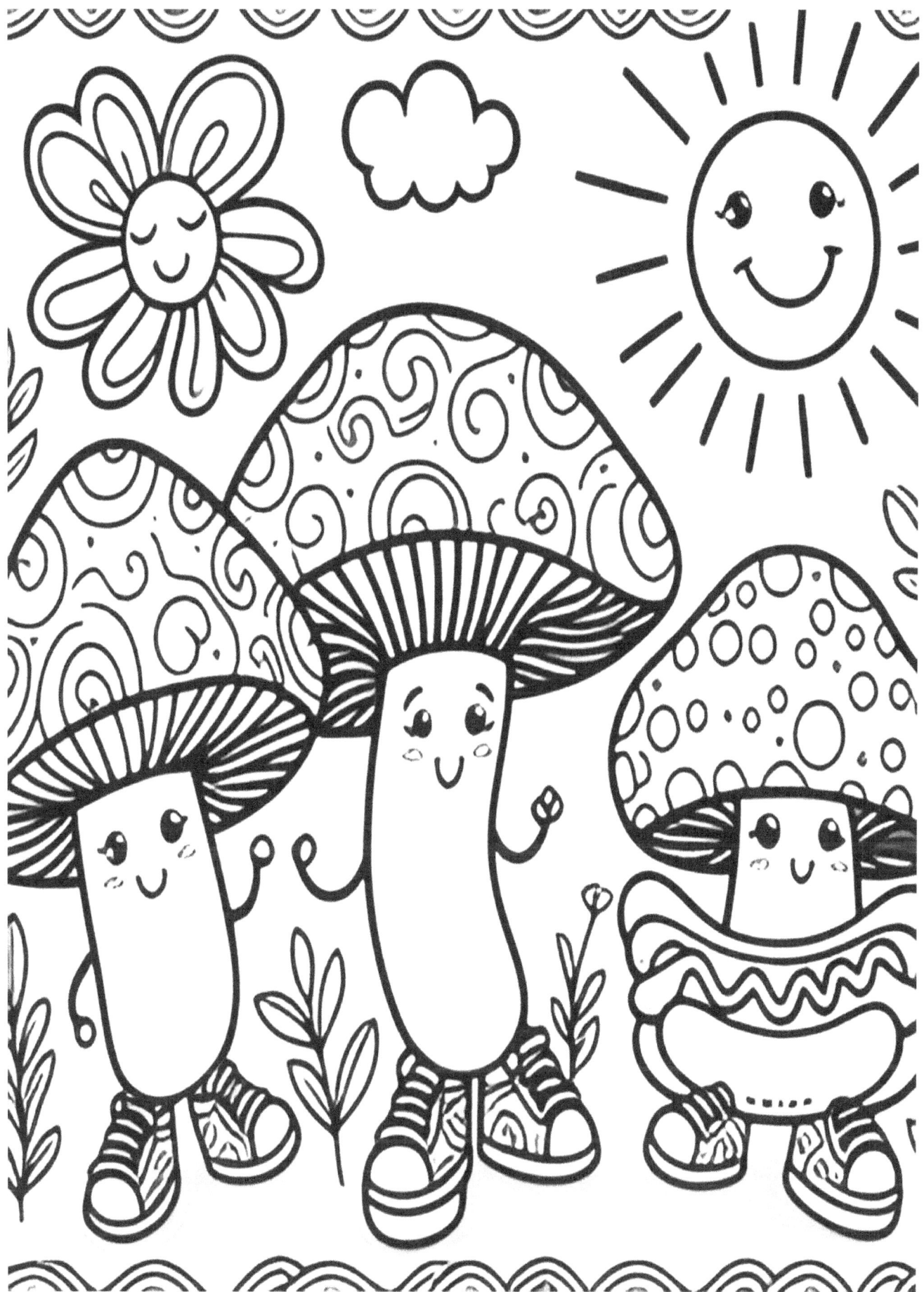

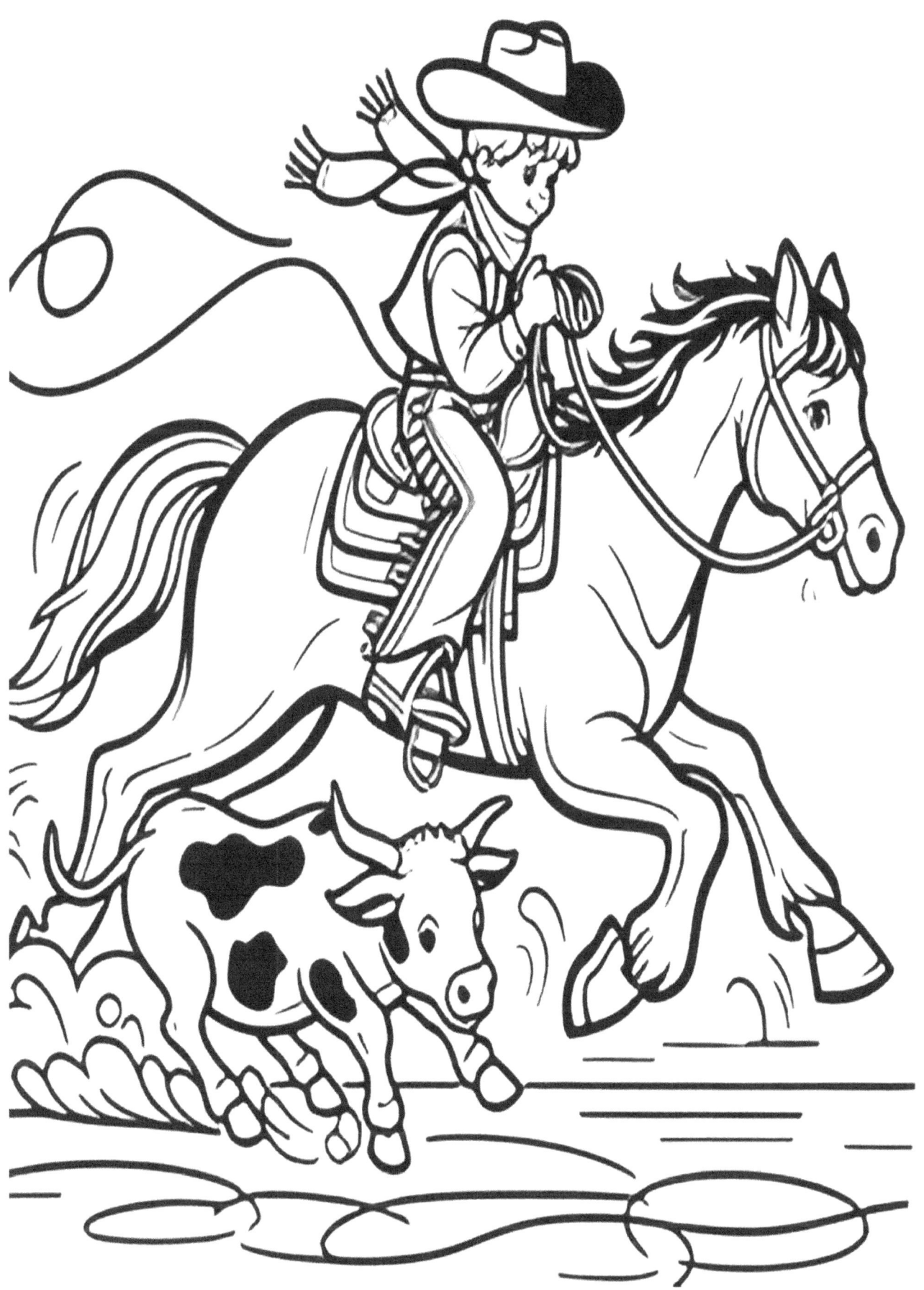

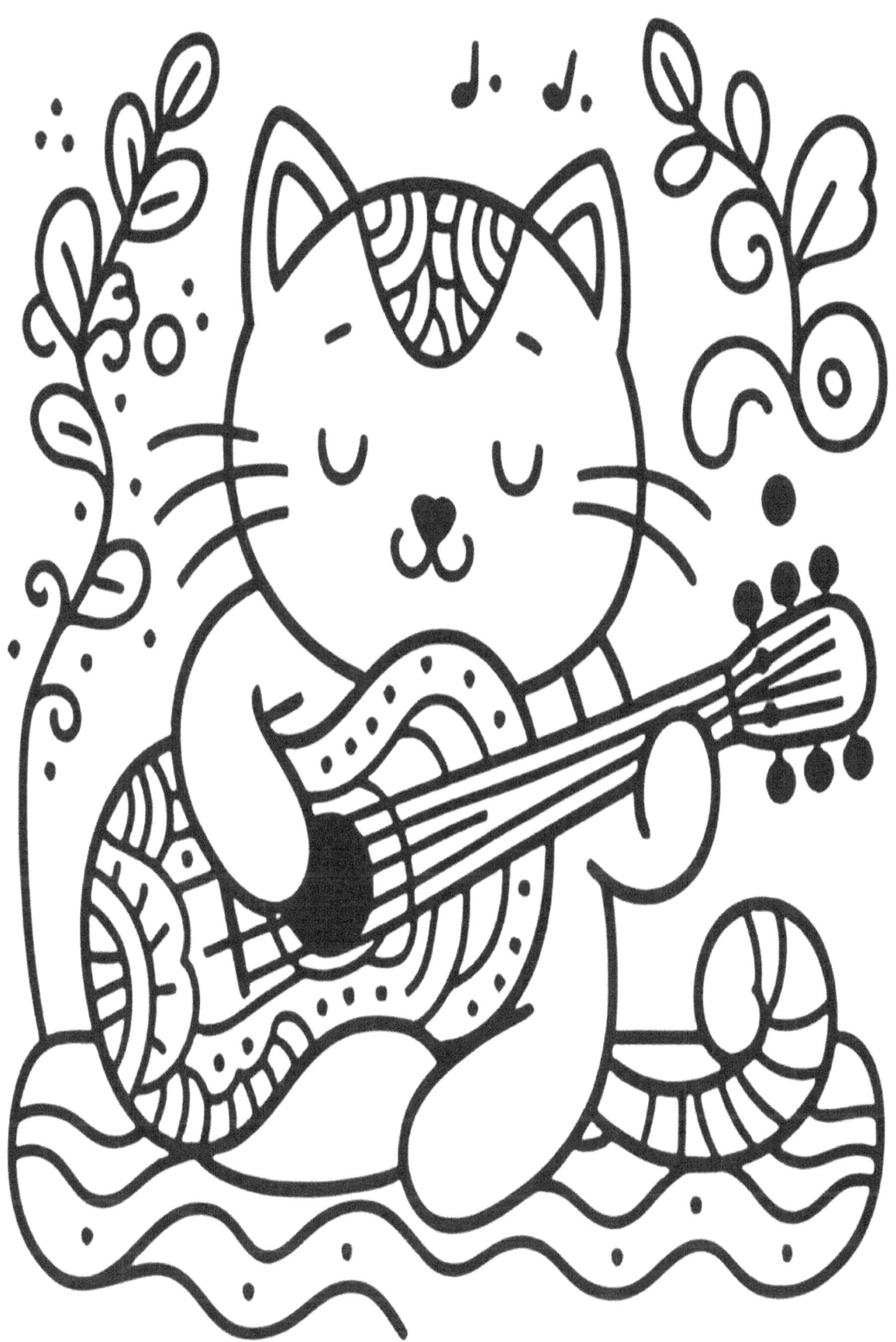

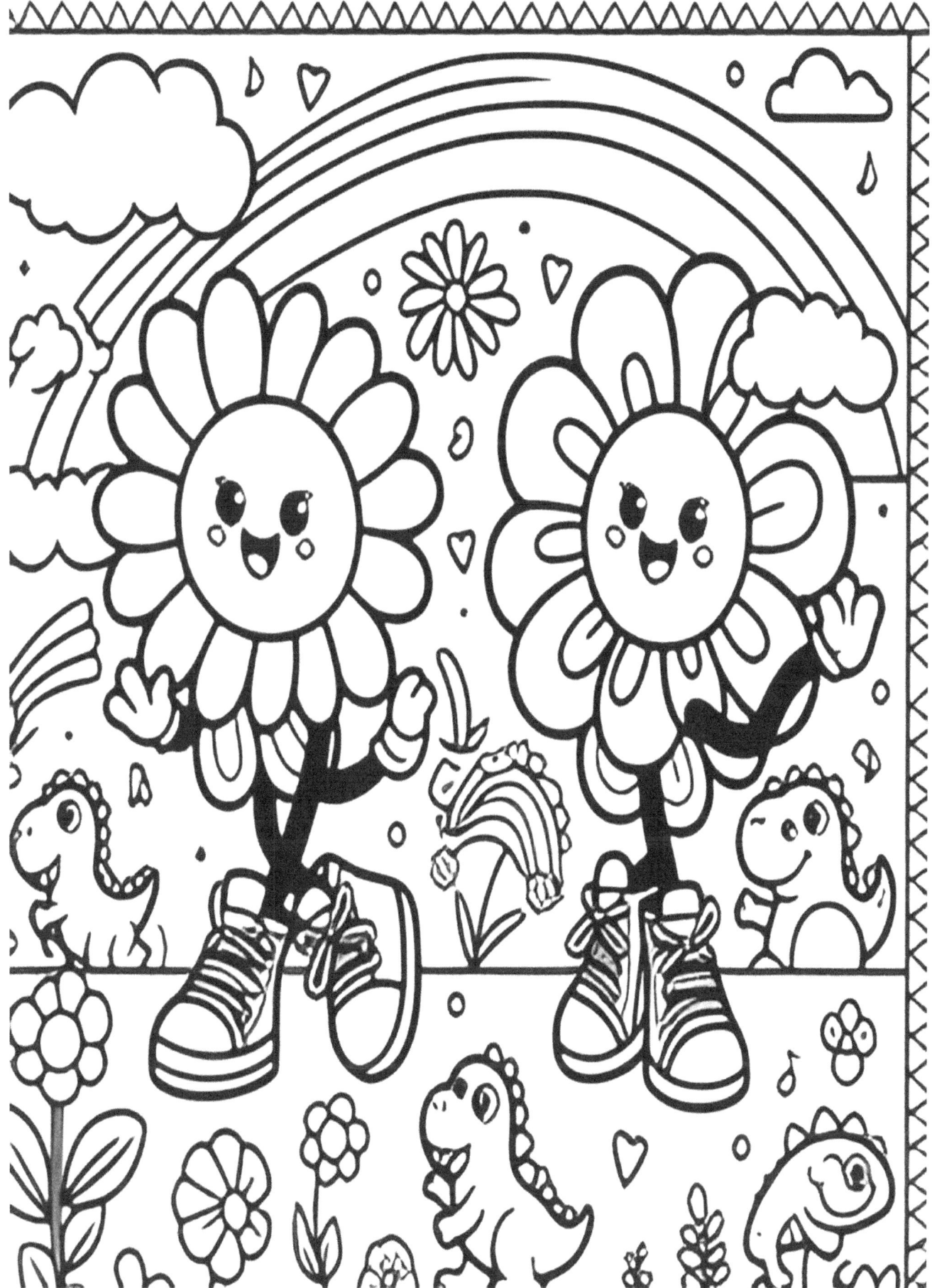

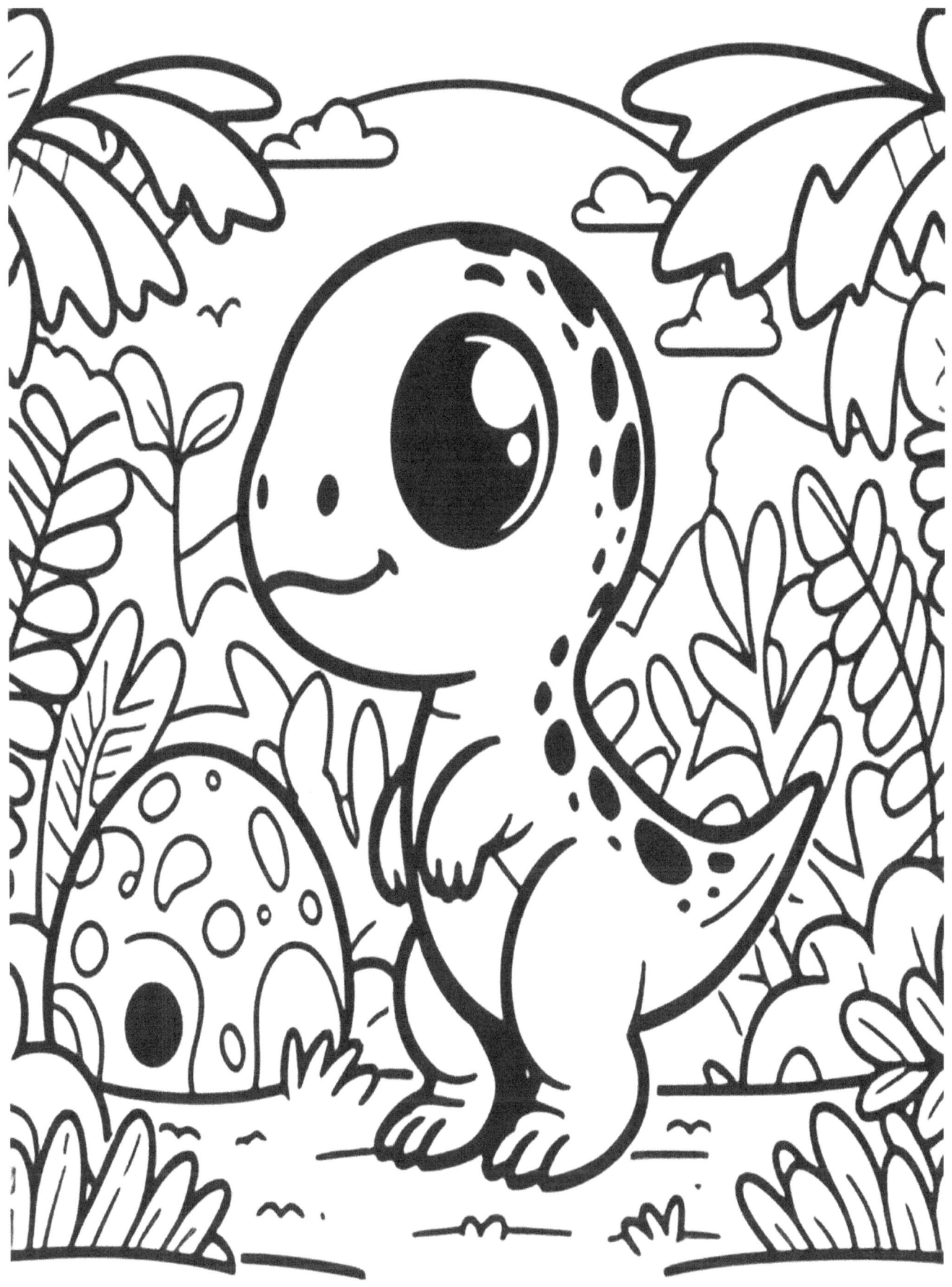

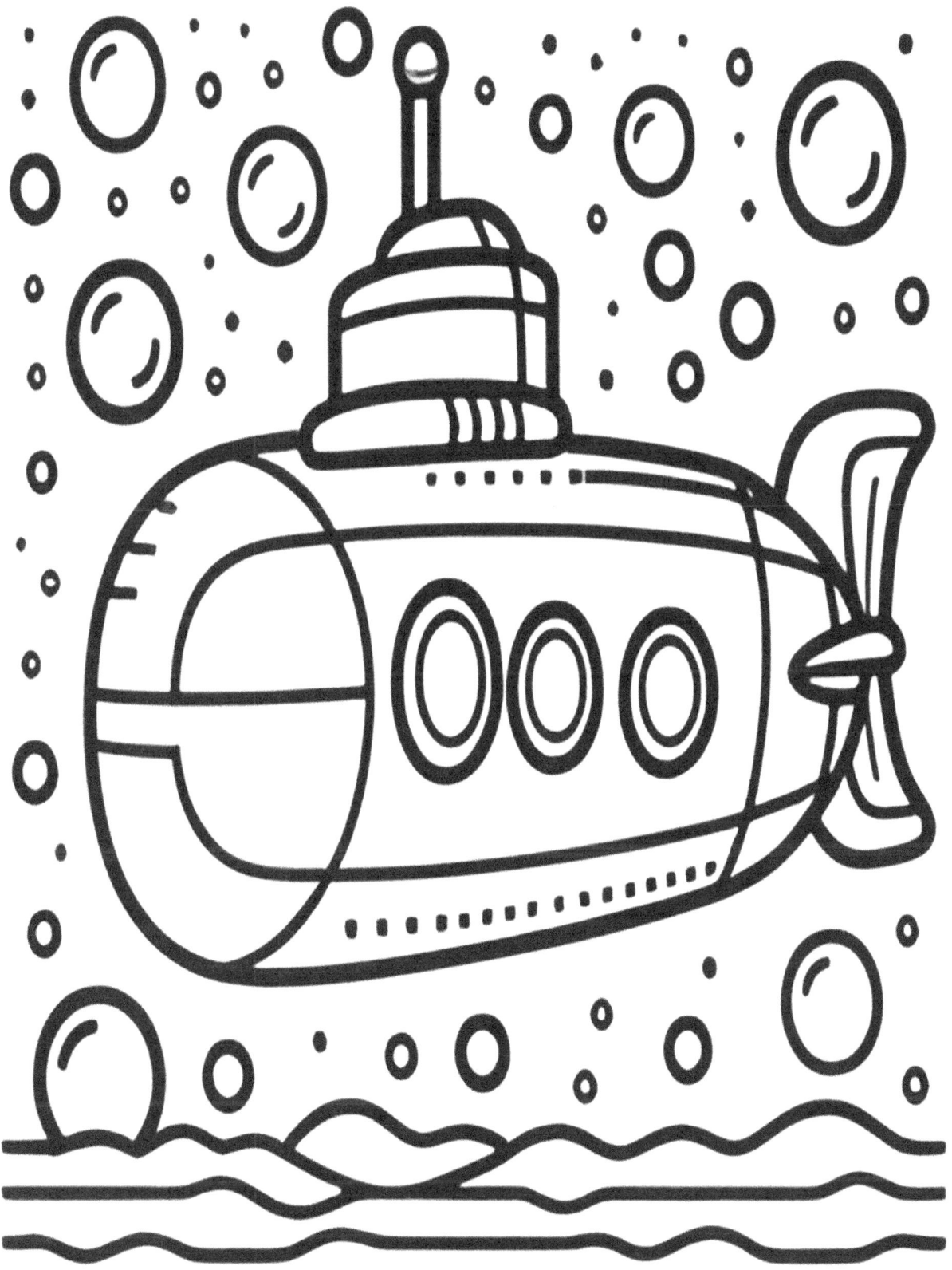

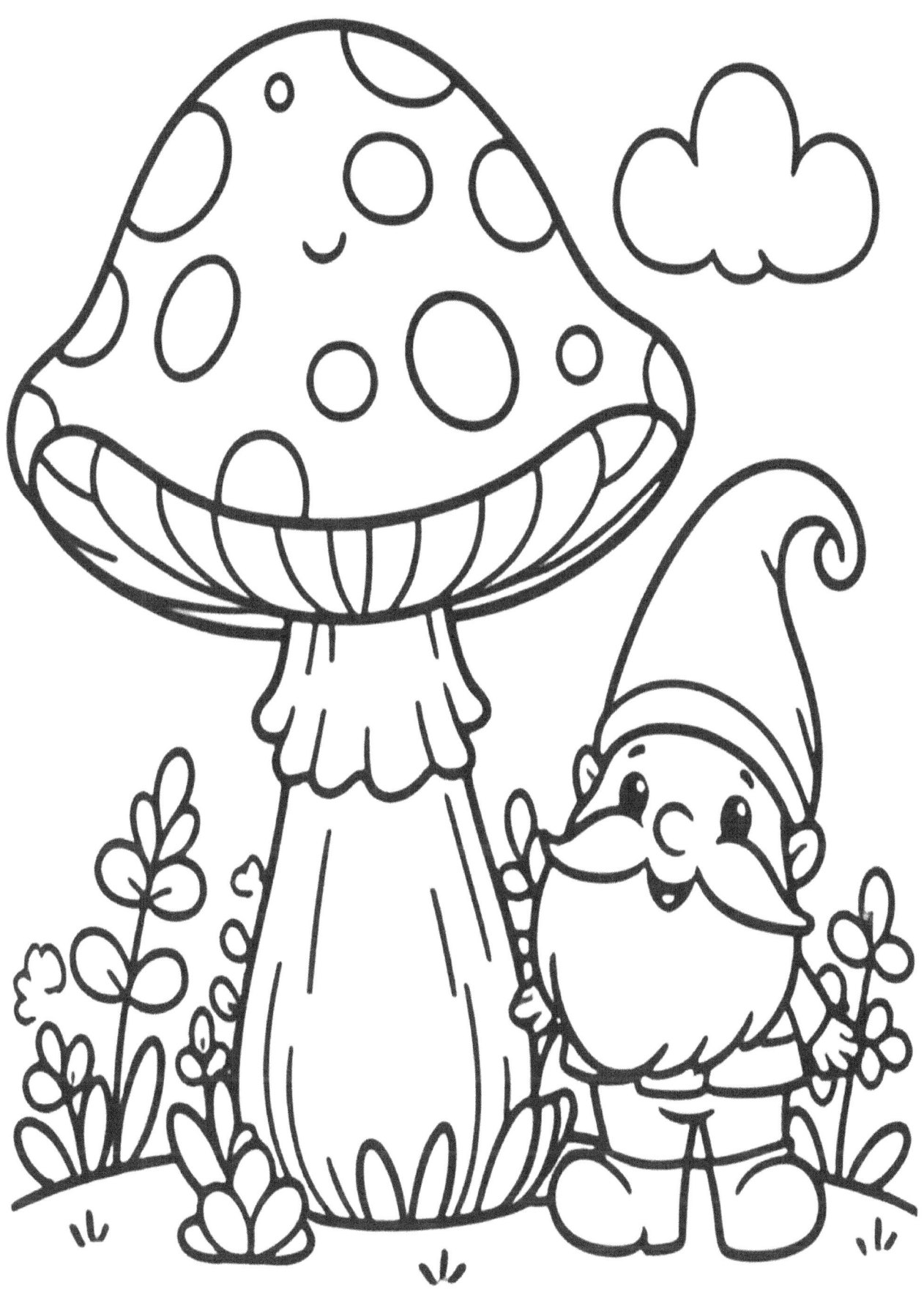

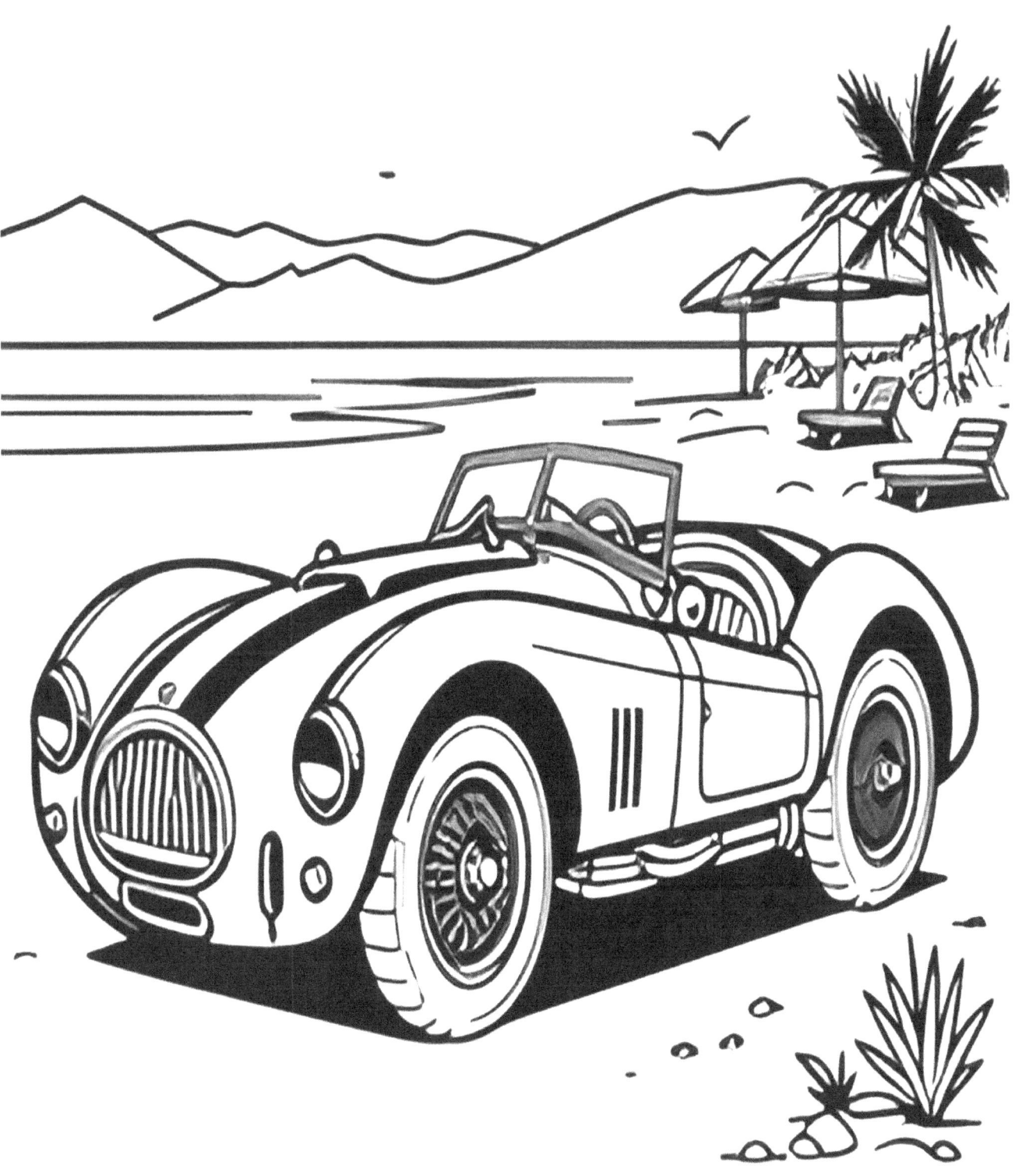

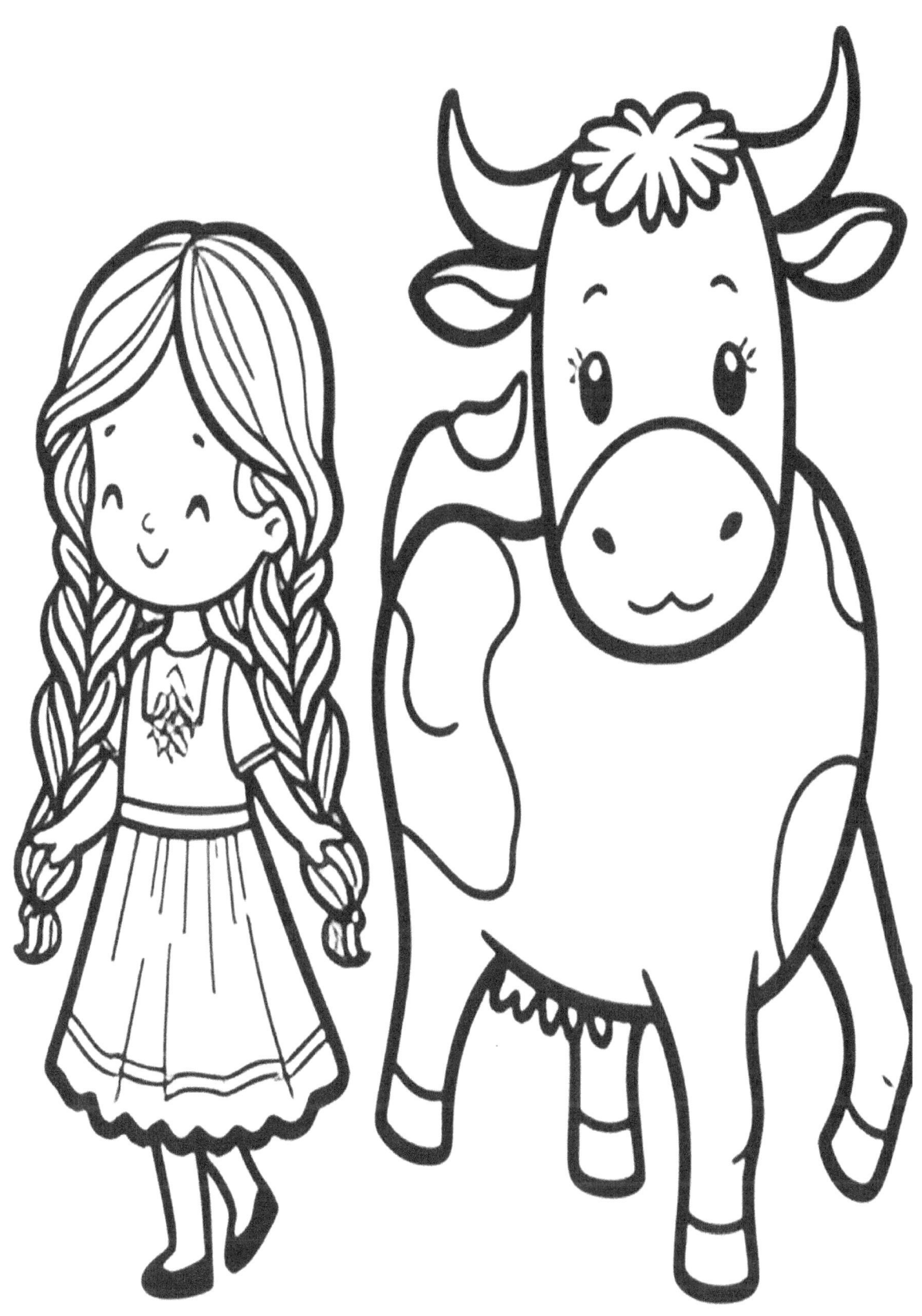

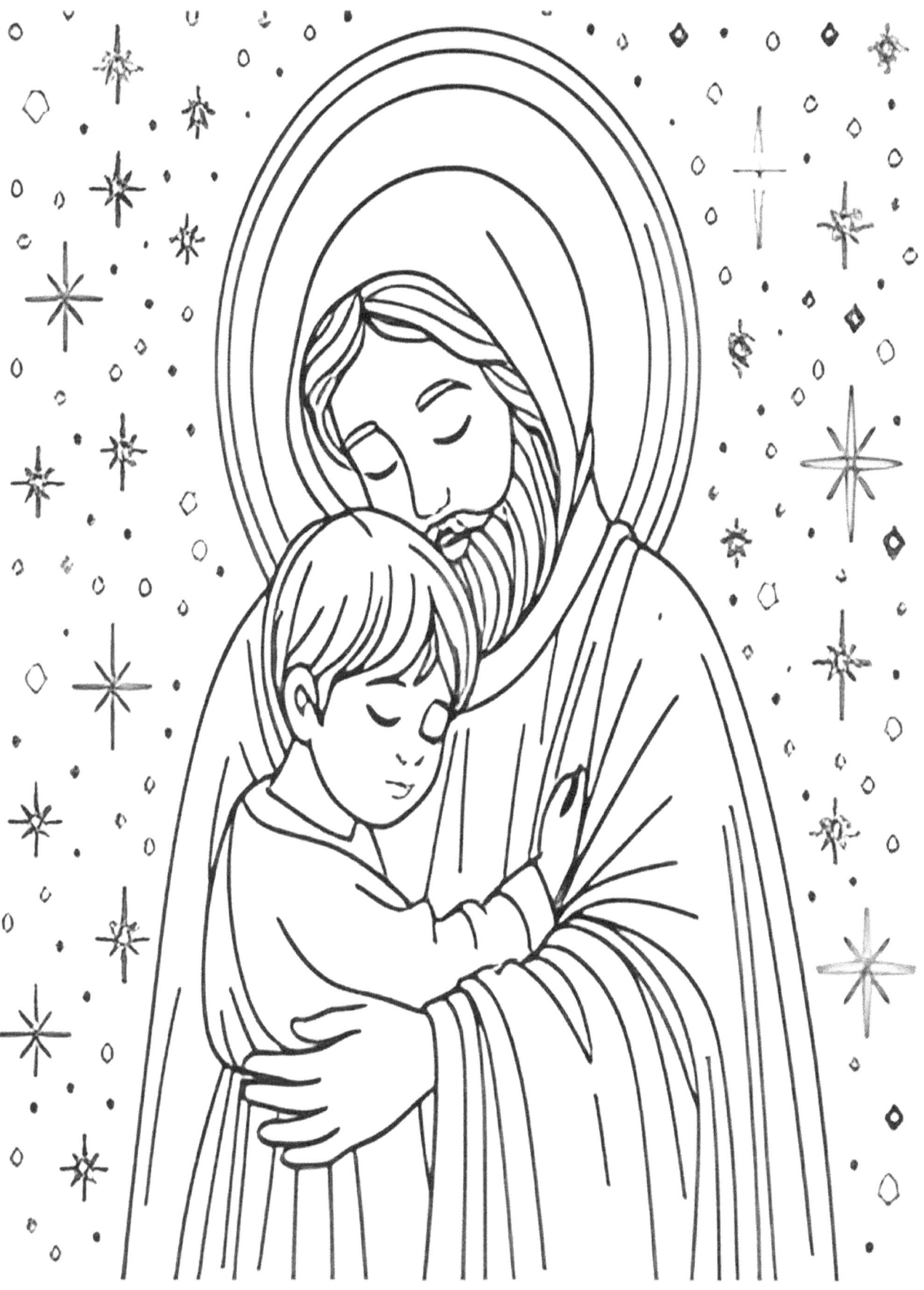

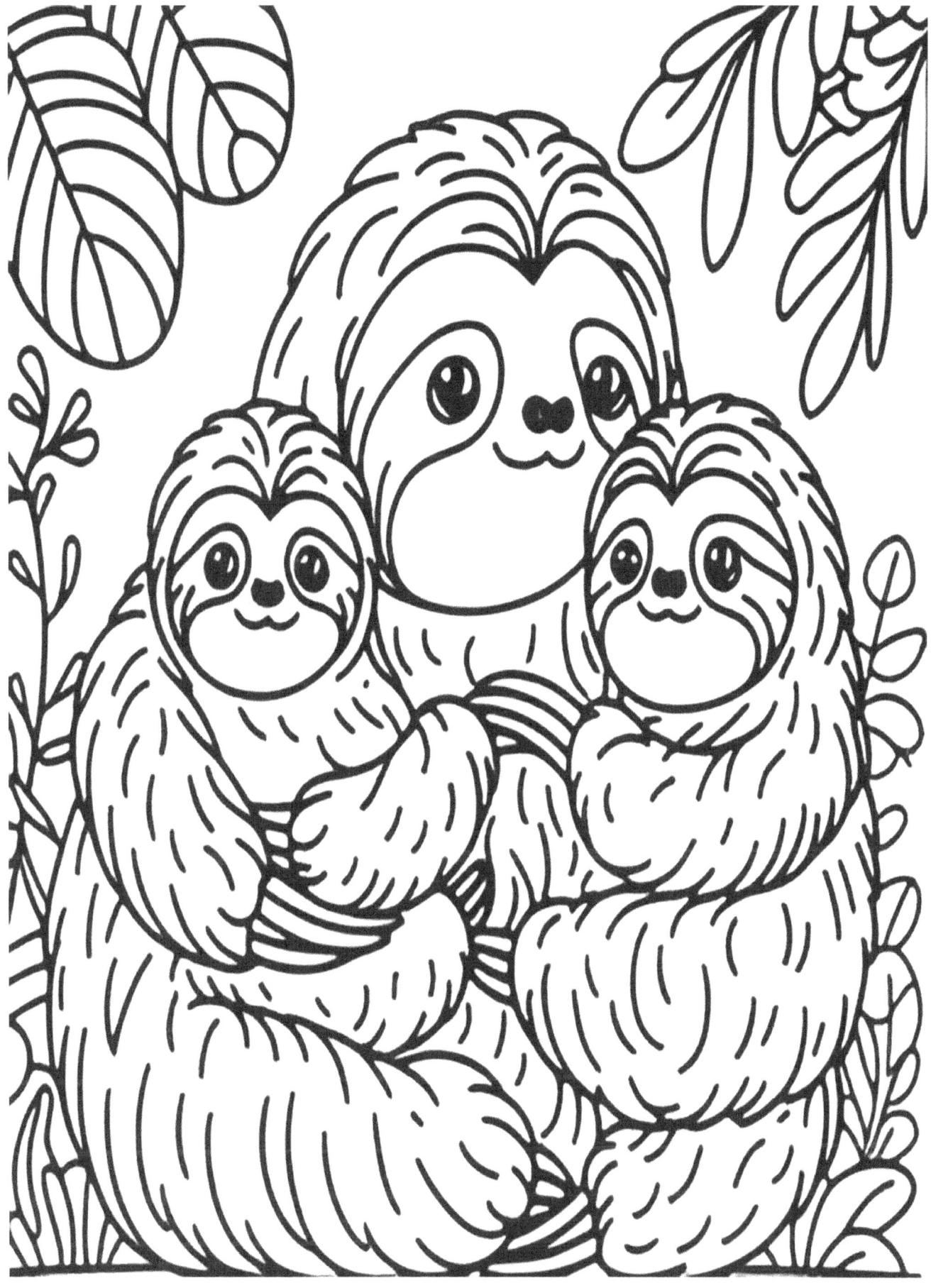

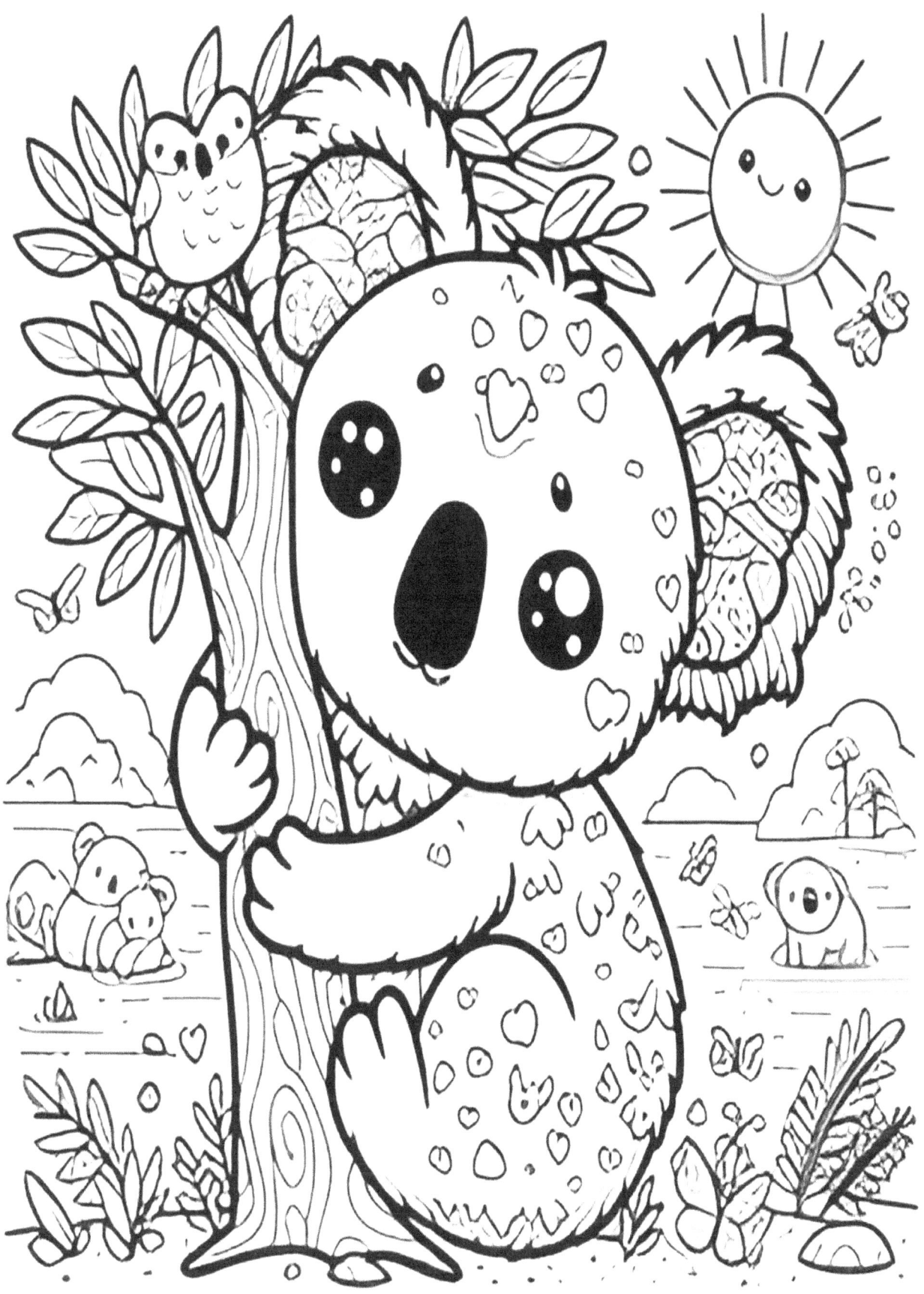

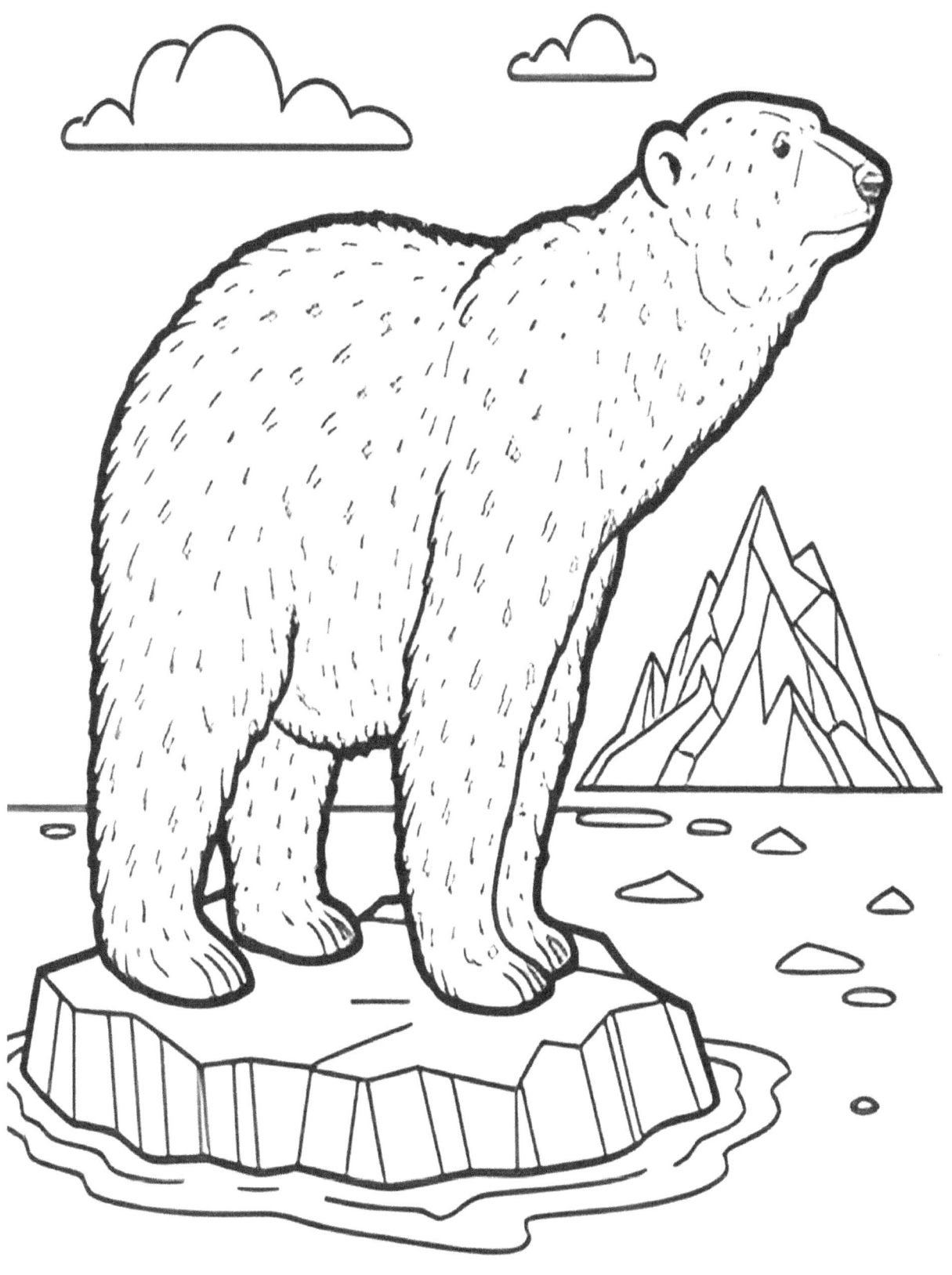

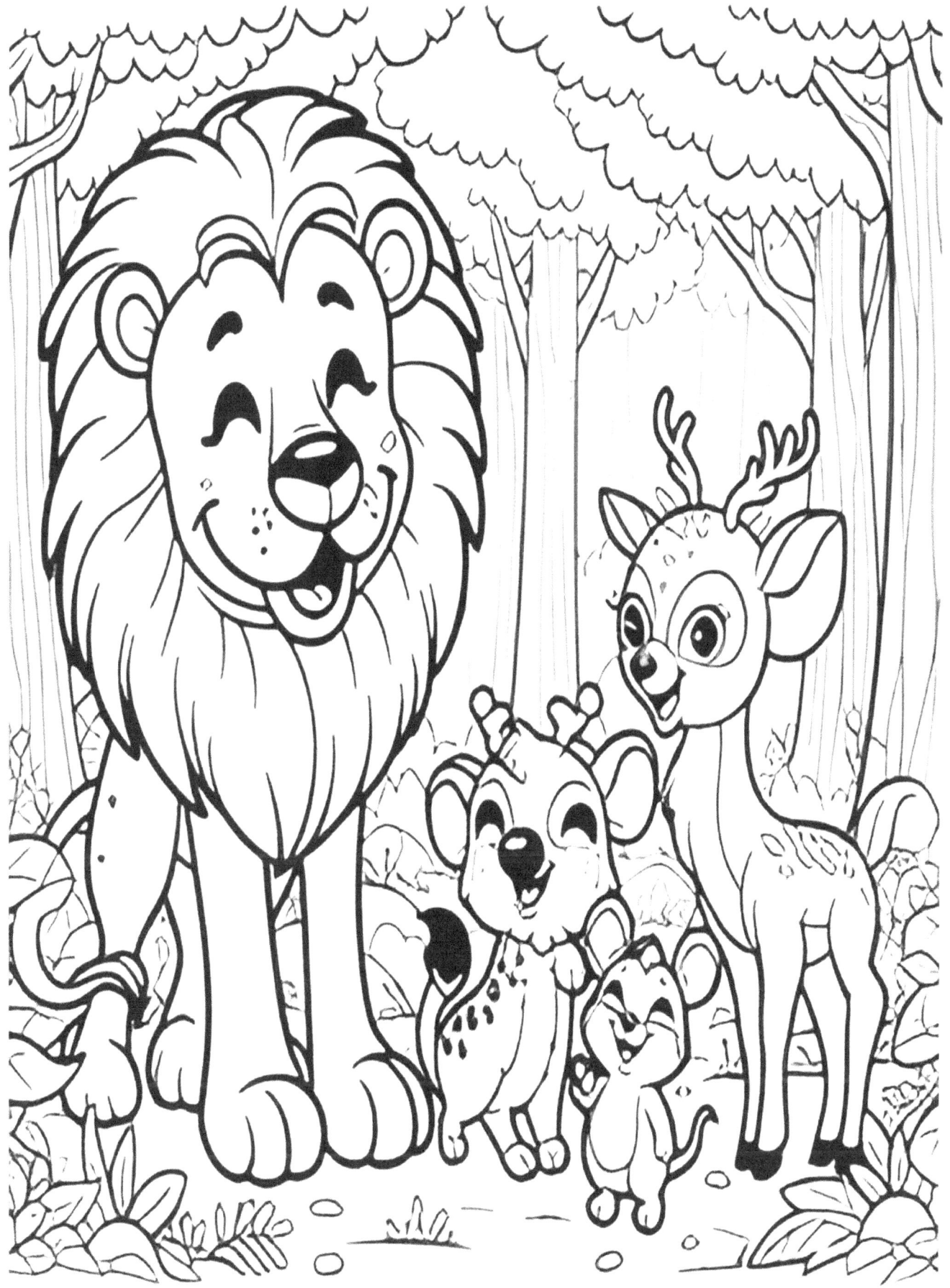

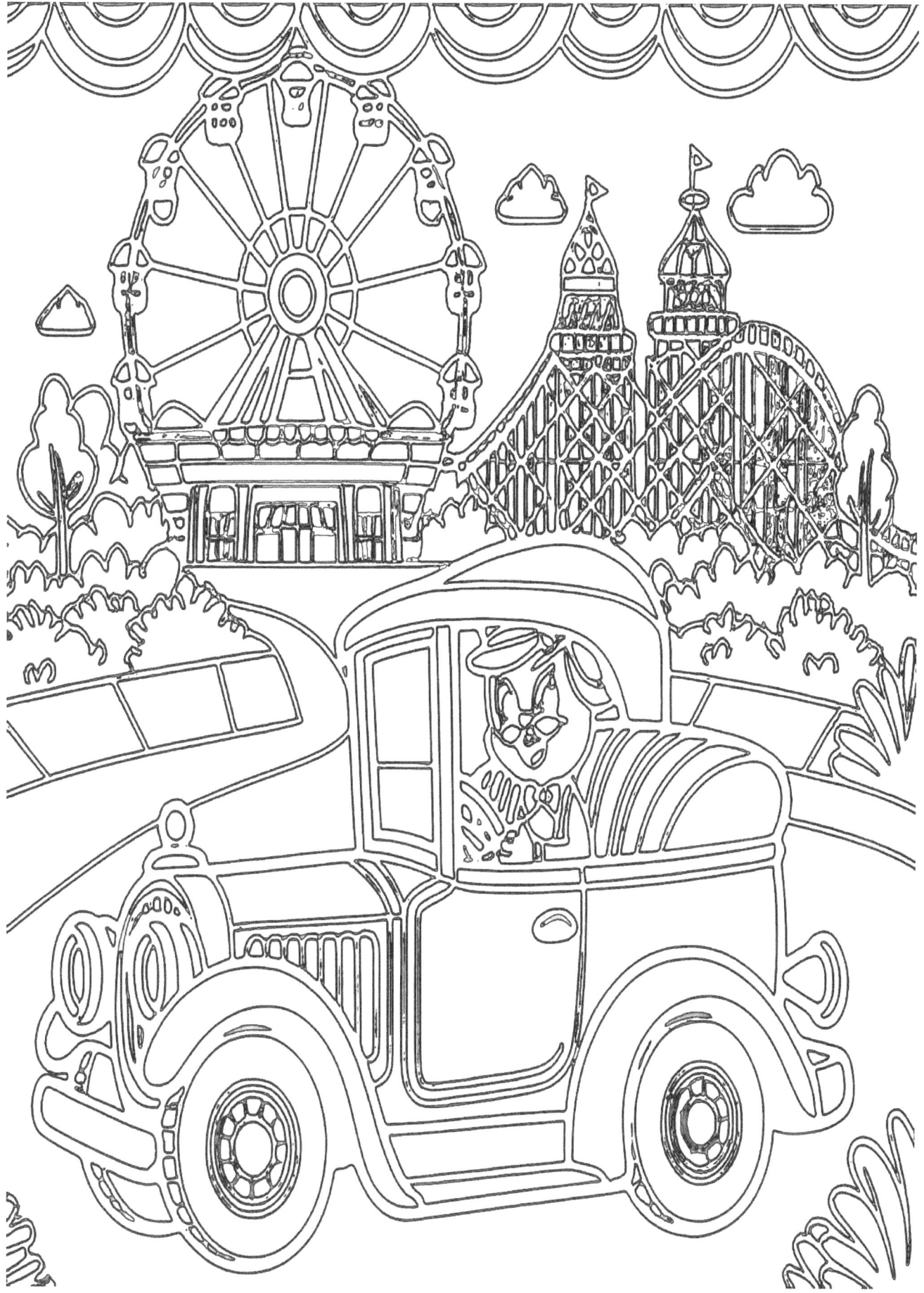

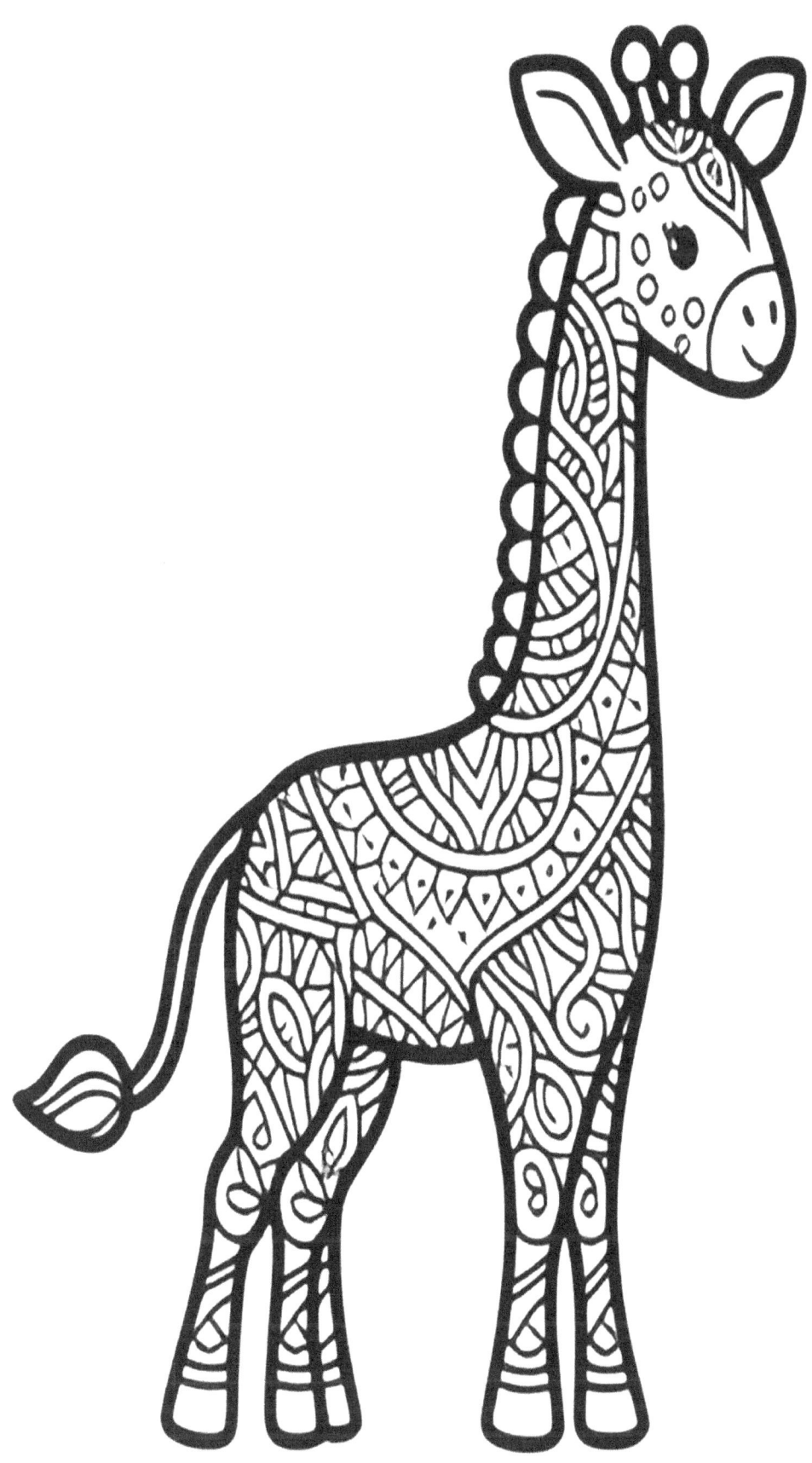

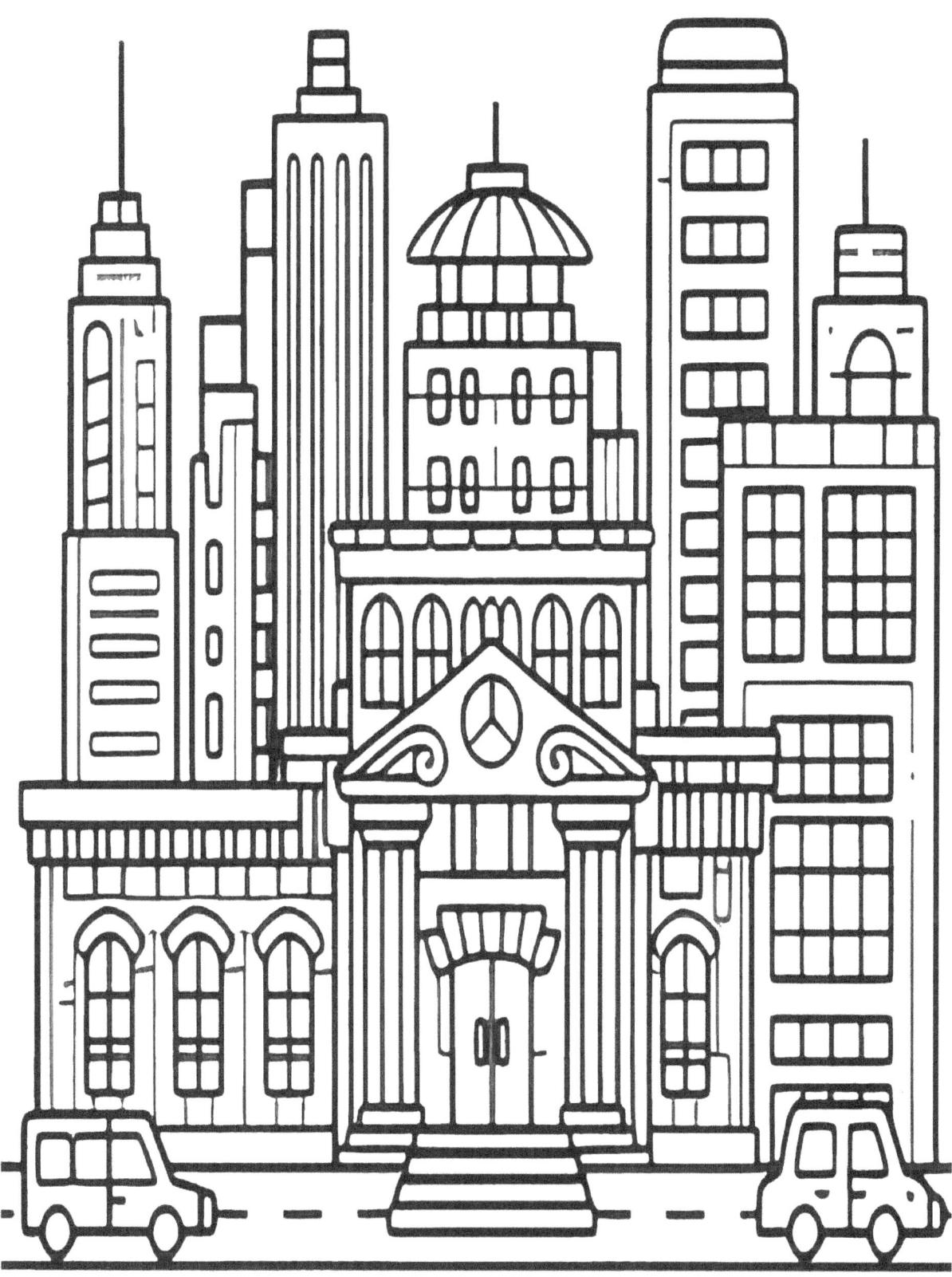

www.ingramcontent.com/pod-product-compliance
Lightning Source LLC
Chambersburg PA
CBHW081119290526
45795CB00006B/2172